For X

ABOUT THE AUTHOR

Emily O'Reilly is the author of *Candidate: The Truth Behind the Presidential Campaign* (Attic Press, 1991). She is Political Correspondent of the *Irish Press* and previously worked for *The Sunday Tribune, Today Tonight* and has contributed to numerous other publications and radio and television programmes.

She won the 'AT Cross Woman Journalist of the Year' Award in 1986 for her coverage of Northern Ireland for *The Sunday Tribune*. In 1987 she was awarded a Nieman Journalism Fellowship at Harvard University, Boston, USA.

Acknowledgements

To Jon O'Brien of the Irish Family Planning Association (IFPA) for access to the IFPA press clippings. To Ruth Riddick for documentation relating to pregnancy counselling in Ireland. To members of the `conservative lobby', particularly Brendan Shortall and Senator Des Hanafin who very kindly and very courteously took the time to talk about their work. To Liam Fay of *Hot Press* magazine for documentation relating to the Knights of St Columbanus and to former Knight Walter Batt for providing the documentation in the first place.

To Stephen and Jessie for putting up with it all.

Finally I would like to thank Attic Press for giving me the go-ahead to the original proposal for this book two years ago.

John O'Reilly refused to give an interview for this book despite two invitations to do so. For that reason I have cited from time to time the work of a writer with whom Mr O'Reilly did co-operate; Tom Hesketh and his work *The Second Partitioning of Ireland*, in my account of the Pro-Life Amendment Campaign.

Permissions:

The publisher gratefully acknowledges permission to quote from:

All In A Life: An Autobiography, by Garret FitzGerald, published by Gill and Macmillan, Dublin, 1991; *Eunuchs For Heaven: the Catholic Church & Sexuality*, by Uta Ranke-Heinemann, published by Andre Deutsch, 1990;

Contents

Mr John O'Reilly

Introduction

The Case Of Sheila Hodgers

This is the story of a very Irish coup.

It is the story of how a state employee hijacked this country's social legislation for almost two decades.

It is the story of how the state's elected representatives, from local councillors to Taoisigh, came to let him do so.

It is the story of how an amendment to our Constitution, intended to place an absolute ban on intentional abortion, became instead the instrument by which abortion was legalised in this state.

It is the story of how a little-known state employee, through the masterful manipulation of successive Governments, emerged to threaten the future of the entire European Community.

It tells of a clash of absolutes - between the right to life of the foetus and the right to liberty of the woman carrying it.

But more than anything, this story is about how the ethos of the catholic church, promoted by the state employee and his followers, featured in the death of a woman called Sheila Hodgers and her new-born baby in 1983.

Her story was first told in September 1983, just days before the country voted to endorse the teaching of the catholic church in relation to abortion. It was told too late to have any effect on the final vote. Retelling it now may give some people pause for thought as the country once again moves to vote in a new abortion referendum.

The story was first told by journalist Padraig Yeates in *The Irish Times* and was never contradicted by the hospital involved. Sheila Hodgers was a young woman, married to Brendan Hodgers and the mother of two children. The family lived in Drogheda, County Louth. In August 1981 Sheila Hodgers detected a lump on her breast. The lump, a cyst, was removed shortly afterwards at Our Lady of Lourdes Hospital in Drogheda.

Sheila's husband, Brendan Hodgers, was later told by the surgeon that a second operation was needed, a mastectomy. A very deep tumour had been found. Without the operation

Sheila would have less than a year to live.

The subsequent operation appeared to have been successful. The all-clear was given. A follow-up course of drugs was prescribed with a warning not to use the contraceptive pill in tandem with the cancer drugs as the hormone preparation in the pill can reactivate cancer of the breast or womb.

Brendan Hodgers later claimed he was told that pregnancy would not be a problem, although the consultant involved has denied that this was the case. Sheila Hodgers, who had not been told of the seriousness of her condition prior to the operation, knew of no reason why she should not get pregnant immediately with a third child.

One year after the operation she did get pregnant. Back at the Lourdes Hospital, she was taken off the anti-cancer drugs. The so-called cytotoxic drugs would kill the developing foetus.

One month after she had been taken off the cancer treatment, Sheila Hodgers began experiencing severe back pains. A reactivated tumour was suspected. By December, Sheila could hardly stand or walk. The family doctor told Brendan Hodgers that he could give her no treatment because of the pregnancy.

For the next few weeks, Brendan Hodgers had a series of talks with the doctors at Lourdes Hospital. He suggested a caesarian section before full term, or an induced delivery. Every proposal was rejected on the grounds that it would damage the foetus. They would not give Sheila Hodgers an X-ray to get an accurate diagnosis of her condition because that too would damage the foetus.

The hospital was bound by an ethical code called the Bishop's Contract, drawn up between hospital management and the catholic hierarchy. Even without it, hospital policy in relation to cases such as Sheila Hodgers would have been the same. Run by an order of Catholic nuns, they believed in the absolute equality of woman and foetus, of preserving both lives. Preserving the foetus, however, involved suspending the woman's cancer treatment. They would not give her painkillers. At the front door of the hospital Brendan Hodgers could hear his wife screaming from her bed on the fourth floor. Mr Hodgers told Padraig Yeates: 'I went to see Sheila one night and she was in absolute agony. She was literally screaming at this stage. I could hear her from the front door of

8

the hospital and she was in a ward on the fourth floor. I saw the sister and she produced a doctor who said nothing that made any sense.'

Transferred to the maternity unit, Sheila was given pain relief and everything possible to at least keep her comfortable.

Brendan Hodgers asked a doctor if she might have an abortion. The doctor did not reply. Sheila Hodgers now wanted to be induced or to have a caesarian section. She insisted the foetus was big enough to be born. The doctors would not do as she asked. They insisted that the baby would not survive if induced now or delivered through caesarian. They simply hoped that she would be able to deliver naturally when the time came.

In the early hours of St Patrick's Day, 17 March 1983, Sheila Hodgers delivered a baby girl. The child, perfectly formed, stopped breathing and died as she emerged from her mother's womb. Sheila Hodgers died two days later. The rights of both could not have been more finely balanced. Mother *and* baby had died.

The Battle Is Joined

The story of this very Irish coup begins almost twenty five years ago in 1968 when a so-called 'Family Planning Study Circle' was set up in Dublin by a small group of doctors. These doctors were determined to give women access to contraception through a loophole in the state's contraception laws. Under Section 17 of the Criminal Law Amendment Act 1935, the sale, advertising and importation for sale of contraceptives was illegal. The doctors could however give them away for free while at the same time requesting 'donations' from their clients.

The Act was backed up by other restrictive legislation including The Customs Consolidation Act 1876, and the Censorship of Publications Act, 1929/1967. The latter Act banned the dissemination of information on contraception.

What was utterly daft and utterly Irish about the law was the absence of either a constitutional or a statutory ban on the *use* of contraceptives. But as they could not be sold or imported, the only way to get legal access to them was apparently to make them yourself or find a kindly doctor willing to give them out for free.

The birth control pill could be imported and sold as this could be used for reasons other than contraception, the regulation of the menstrual cycle, for example. And in Ireland, to judge from the number of birth control pills sold, an extraordinary number of women happened to need their cycles regulated!

The 1935 Act was a classic of its kind, enacted by Eamon de Valera's Government as part of a process of asserting the country's 'independence' from pagan England. To be really Irish, went the thinking at the time, it was necessary to be both Republican and Roman Catholic.

Two years later, in 1937, the special position accorded to the catholic church was sewn into the Constitution with the only voice of protest in the Oireachtas, that of poet and Senator WB Yeats.

In 1968 very large families were still the norm in many Irish households. Families of twelve, fifteen, even twenty plus children were not uncommon and many women could expect to spend most of their adult lives pregnant or completely housebound by the demands of young and teenage children.

10

The consequences for a woman's health and life expectancy through repeated pregnancies were enormous. For many women, breastfeeding, with its acknowledged but highly erratic contraceptive effect, provided the only respite between pregnancies. Sterilisation for non-medical purposes was, and still is, forbidden in the catholic run hospitals.

The option of working outside the home was unrealistic even without the demands of the family. In 1933 new legislation, again enacted by de Valera's Government, had required women teachers to resign on marriage, though this was repealed some years later, presumably because of the lack of substitute male teachers.

In 1935, ministerial powers were given to prohibit totally or to limit the number of women employed in a particular industry. And, until 1973, a ban was imposed on the employment of married women in the civil service, local authorities and health boards. Women were forced to resign on marriage, although some were allowed to return to temporary, lower-paid posts if they wished.

Those who did work received less money than their married male counterparts and the exceptional women who rose to the top in either business or the professions tended not to marry. The state conspired to ensure that you could not 'have it all'.

Even in the late 1960s and early 1970s, that great period of female emancipation, the Irish state was legally forcing women to conform to de Valera's constitutional ideal of a woman contributing to the state solely through her work in the home.

The ban on contraception invariably meant that women had so many children they couldn't work outside the home anyway. And even if they did get around this through abstinence or rigid adherence to the 'safe period', a huge chunk of the employment market was closed off once you were married.

Add to that the corresponding forced economic dependence on one's husband through the lack of family home protection legislation and you had a situation where women quite literally were enslaved.

The state's ban on contraception was central to the realisation in Ireland of the catholic church's grand plan for the role of women in society. That role should be confined, for

11

married women at least, to the domestic sphere. They should be actively prevented from playing a role in the public affairs of the nation.

Some catholic thinkers took an even more warped view of the benefits that accrued to men from denying women control of their fertility. In the recently published germinal work on the catholic church and matters sexual, *Eunuchs for Heaven*, by German Theologian Uta Ranke-Heinemann, the author quotes a passage from an article published in 1976 in an Italian diocesan newspaper. It reads: 'Because of women's increased life expectancy - their average age at death in the last century was only thirty-five, and many of them, debilitated by frequent childbirth, died in childbed itself - the number of couples who live together for thirty, fifty, or even sixty years has also increased. This longevity entails an additional test for the husband in particular. The death of a man's wife, often at an early age, at one time enabled him to contract a new and legitimate marriage with another, usually younger, woman, whereas he is now compelled to make do with a wife who often ages faster than himself.'

Uta Ranke-Heineman comments : 'So everyone has a cross to bear: woman has been robbed of freedom by the pill and rendered 'usable', man is robbed of freedom by his wife's advancing age. The pill has contributed to this male affliction because fewer women are so debilitated by frequent childbirth that they die in the process, thereby vacating the marriage bed in favour of younger successors.'

A great deal of sentiment was also attached to large families in Ireland, a covert way of telling mothers that a life of unrelenting drudgery was a noble and wonderful thing, and of encouraging others to please copy.

Such families occasionally featured on TV programmes such as *The Late Late Show* accompanied by admiring gasps from the audience, risqué comments thrown at the now publicly acknowledged (and beaming) stud of a father and a few patronising remarks bounced off the invariably stoic and exhausted woman. This then was her reward: a public and entirely useless commendation for lying back and doing it all for Ireland.

Some years ago a woman from Dublin's working class inner city area, described on *The Late Late Show* how she had given birth to, and reared, nine or ten children while still holding down a full time job as a cleaner or waitress in a city centre theatre. What was astonishing about her story was that she had managed to conceal her pregnancies from her employers who believed her to be a single woman. She feared the loss of her job if she told them she was married with children. (In fact the management did not follow this course of action when they discovered her secret.)

She would organise her annual two weeks leave to coincide with the expected birth. On the day her labour began, she would simply wait till her shift was over, walk home (yes, walk home) along the quays, spread newspapers on her bed and lie down and wait for the midwife or doctor to deliver her. Two weeks later she would report back to work, the new child presumably farmed out to a relative or neighbour or an older sibling.

Great gales of laughter and applause greeted her story. No one paused to consider the awfulness of the woman's plight; the forced concealment of her pregnancies, the potential damage to her and to her foetus' health as she worked right up to labour day.

It was to alleviate the plight of women in similar conditions that the Family Planning Study Circle was founded in 1968. This was followed in February 1969 by a small revolution - the opening at 10 Merrion Square of the Fertility Guidance Clinic - the first private clinic in the history of the state to offer contraceptive advice and help.

Before that, family planning clinics operated only in the larger maternity hospitals and they advised only on the church-approved rhythm method. Demand for advice on even that was so intense that the hospital clinics were forced to limit their services to maternity patients of the hospital only.

In 1968 the Coombe Hospital had closed its clinic. Some time later, Father Michael Browne, a curate in Harold's Cross, established a Dublin diocesan family counselling service. The service would include, however, advice only on 'natural methods'.

Meanwhile the privately owned clinic went ahead. The directors of the Fertility Guidance Company Ltd included Dr James T Loughran, Dr Michael Solomons with a practice at Fitzwilliam Square, Dr Dermot Hourihane, Dr RP Towers, Dr Joan Wilson, Maire Mullarney a nurse and mother of eleven, and Yvonne Pim a social worker.

Some of those involved later became active in the 1983 campaign, opposed to the proposed insertion of the anti-abortion amendment into the Constitution.

The language used by the directors to describe their services was most circumspect given the range of legal and social forces hostile to their agenda. Advice was to be given to married or, daringly, to 'engaged' couples. But even newspaper reports declined to spell out the types of contraception available.

Hibernia magazine reported: 'Each consultation is a very thorough matter. The patient is medically examined, and her gynaecological history is investigated; this process may well suggest the unsuitability of some methods of birth control. She is then asked if she - or her husband, who is usually present during the interview - has a religious, aesthetic or practical objection to other methods which are discussed. The alternative methods left after processes of elimination are then considered in detail, a final choice is made and the appropriate prescription written.'

In fact the only legal contraceptive the doctors could prescribe, or even get their hands on, was the pill. Clients had to get condoms, diaphragms and spermicidal jelly either from Northern Ireland or by post from a despatch office in London. Clients opting for the intra-uterine device were referred to a doctor in Belfast attached to the Northern Ireland Family Planning association.

One other significant allegation emerged from reports of the new clinic; that it was funded in part by the International Planned Parenthood Federation (IPPF), an organisation which believes that planned parenthood is an expression of people's free choice in regulating their fertility, and that individuals and families should be provided with the means to achieve it. And those means included the termination of pregnancy through abortion.

The IPPF, according to newspaper reports, had paid for the renovation of the premises at Merrion Square. The extent of general public knowledge about the IPPF at that time was negligible, but the report of its involvement in the new clinic put those individuals and groups hostile to the promotion and legalisation of contraception on red alert and in later years the IPPF was targeted as the *bête noire* of the anti-contraception and anti-abortion lobbies.

In September 1969 two representatives from the clinic became the first Irish representatives ever to attend the IPPF annual congress in Budapest. A fundamental change in the country's approach to contraception was now quietly underway. The new clinic was operating openly. In addition, the first hesitant, legislative steps were being made to repeal the restrictions on contraception. 1971 witnessed a failed attempt by Independent Senators Mary Robinson (now President of Ireland), Trevor West and John Horgan to bring in a Private Members Bill to allow for the importation and sale of contraceptives.

But in March of that year the backlash began. That month, a pastoral letter from the then Archbishop of Dublin and Primate of Ireland, the late John Charles McQuaid, denounced artificial methods of contraception, stating that any successful attempt to legalise them would result in 'a curse upon the land'. He wrote: 'It may well come to pass that in the present climate of emotional thinking and pressure, legislation would be enacted that will offend the objective moral law. Such a measure would be an insult to our faith; it would without question prove to be gravely damaging to morality, private and public; it would be, and would remain, a curse upon our country.'

But outside of that no real attempt was made by pressure groups or by the state authorities to put the fledgling clinic out of business, though directors claimed that efforts were made to frustrate the importation of certain contraceptives and in 1970 the then Attorney General had rejected pressure from certain unnamed quarters to take a prosecution against the clinic.

A new family planning centre was now set up in Mountjoy Square catering for low-income families and the clinic directors finally summoned the nerve to substitute the unwieldy Fertility Guidance Company Ltd for the title Irish Family Planning Association (IFPA). Contraception had now officially come of age in Ireland.

Enter John O'Reilly

In 1973 the so-far undisturbed pace of change on the birth control front would be challenged. And in 1973 would emerge the man, that state employee, whose machinations on behalf of the conservative catholic lobby throughout the following two decades would lead directly not just to the insertion of a constitutional ban on abortion in 1983, but also to the defeat of the divorce referendum three years later and to a major threat to the ratification of a new EC treaty six years after that.

It is not an overblown claim. As a colleague of the man put it to the author: 'All trails lead back to O'Reilly...' The man's name is John O'Reilly, otherwise known as Eoghan O Raghallaigh. In newspaper letters through the last two decades he has used both names, presumably to divert attention from the frequency of his correspondence.

He is now middle-aged, an engineer employed by Dublin Corporation. Married with five children he lives in Dalkey, County Dublin. His present associates claim to know little of his early background. They describe him as a good family man, who has a warm and loving relationship with his children. He has, they say, a great sense of humour, a nice line in self-deprecation and a passion for the promotion of his fundamentalist beliefs.

He is a big man, slightly stooped, wears thick-lensed glasses which convey the impression of a squint. This unprepossessing appearance belies totally, and deliberately, the extent of the man's power and the range of his contacts. His political, business and ecclesiastical access is said to be formidable.

Incredibly, for a man who has wielded such covert but effective power for the last two decades, he has never been profiled and very rarely interviewed. He maintains strict media silence, remaining at the back of press conferences when new campaigns are being launched, caught only glancingly by the photographers' lenses as they move to capture the front men and women.

But John O'Reilly was inside Mount Carmel Hospital in Dublin when the founding conference of the Pro-Life Amendment Campaign (PLAC) was held in 1981; he was inside the Four Courts when the Society for the Protection of the Unborn Child (SPUC) sought to ban abortion counselling and information; he was inside the Four Courts when SPUC sought to ban the publication and dissemination of abortion literature; he was inside the Royal Marine Hotel in Dun Laoghaire when the catholic lay organisation Family Solidarity was hatched; he was inside Buswell's Hotel when the Anti-

Divorce Campaign was launched; he was inside Leinster House during the period when the Maastricht abortion protocol was being surreptitiously drawn up; and he was back in Buswell's Hotel when the new, 1992, Pro-Life Campaign was being launched. John O'Reilly was on the inside all the way because he was orchestrating everything that was taking place.

And one day back in 1973 he was sitting at home with his eight-year-old daughter in Dalkey, armed with a writing pad and a postal order planning the first steps of his plot to close down the family planning clinic in 10 Merrion Square.

But John O'Reilly's actions of that year must be seen in the context of two crucial court cases that also took place in 1973, one in Ireland, the other in the United States of America. The cases together provided O'Reilly and others with a framework and focus for action over the next nineteen years.

Roe v Wade and McGee v The Attorney General

The USA case was the landmark Roe v Wade judgement in which the Supreme Court ruled that, except in narrow circumstances, the Constitution of the United States of America does not permit the Government to interfere with a woman's right to choose abortion.

Prior to that ruling individual states had been free to enact their own abortion legislation, allowing it to be as liberal or as restrictive as the state wished. The state also had the option to prohibit abortion outright, an option banned by the Roe v Wade decision.

'Jane Roe' was the pseudonym used by the woman taking the case, Norma McCorvey from Texas. Henry Wade was the real name of a Dallas county prosecutor whose name appeared on one side of the 'versus' in scores of cases, defending the laws of Texas. In 1973 Texas law pledged to uphold the right to life of the foetus. Only in cases where the woman's life was threatened could abortions be carried out.

'Jane Roe's' or Norma McCorvey's story was that she had been gang raped when coming home from work one summer evening in 1969. She was twenty-five years old. Several weeks later she discovered she was pregnant. (A decade and a half after the case she confessed that she hadn't been raped at all. She had become pregnant through consensual sex but was afraid to say so.)

Abortion was illegal where she lived and she lacked the money to travel to another state. She went ahead with the pregnancy but challenged the Texan law nonetheless. In January 1973 the Supreme Court ruled that as part of her constitutional fundamental right to privacy, a woman has the right to terminate her pregnancy. It was a decision that would lead to abortion on demand, at least in the first twelve weeks of pregnancy, throughout the United States of America. The ruling was an extension of a 1965 decision which established the use of contraception as a constitutional right under the right to privacy clause.

Meanwhile, one year earlier in Ireland, a similar case on the right of access to contraception had been heard in the High Court (McGee v The Attorney General). The case was taken by a twenty-seven year old mother of four children, Mary McGee. She did not want any more children. She had had strokes in each of her last two pregnancies and her doctor did not think she should go on the pill.

As sterilisation was virtually impossible to obtain, Mrs McGee's doctor prescribed a diaphragm and spermicides and these were duly despatched from London. The diaphragm, coming by letter mail, got through. But the spermicides were confiscated by the customs authorities under the 1935 Act. Mrs McGee, who lived with her fisherman husband and four children in a caravan trailer in Skerries, County Dublin, thought that this confiscation infringed their rights as a family and appealed to the High Court against the action.

She lost the case. The High Court president, Mr Justice O'Keeffe, said that the law did not outlaw the use of contraceptives, simply their sale and importation and therefore this did not breach her constitutional rights. How Mrs McGee was actually meant to use contraceptives if she could neither buy them at home nor import them was never explained in the court.

The Supreme Court Appeal was heard in November 1973, marked by intense public and media interest. Mrs McGee's senior counsel was the late Seán McBride. In her submission, in addition to the constitutional rights she believed had been violated, Mary McGee referred to US Surpreme Court rulings which had held that certain state laws against contraception were unconstitutional as they were an invasion of privacy.

After several days of wrangling over the extent to which the state could legislate for what goes on in the marital bed, and what acts the constitutional right to privacy covered, the Supreme Court found in favour of Mary McGee. On 19 December 1973, by a majority decision of four judges to one, the court held that the state ban on the importation of contraceptives for personal use was unconstitutional, partly on the grounds that it breached the right to privacy.

The ban on the sale and promotion remained, however, but, as summarised by *Irish Times* writer Dr David Nowlan, the judgement 'chipped the first chunk of mortar out of the legal wall against contraception in Ireland'.

The First O'Reilly Challenge

For anyone set against the relaxation of the contraceptive laws, the events that took place between 1969 and 1973 were alarming. Two attempts had been made to put Bills to that effect before the Oireachtas; the Supreme Court had established that the Constitution allowed, as a personal right, the freedom to import contraceptives for personal use; the USA Supreme Court had used that same constitutional right as a justification for abortion; several family planning clinics were now operating unimpeded, providing consultations at a rate of 12,000 a year; and an information booklet on contraception had survived three sell-out printings without a word from the Censorship of Publications Board.

And across the water in Britain, the 1861 Offences Against the Person Act, the same Act which banned abortion in Ireland, had been repealed in 1967, giving women liberal access to abortion in that country.

In addition, the junior partners in the new Fine Gael/Labour Coalition had declared themselves in favour of the liberalisation of the contraception laws and one year later, in 1974, yet another Private Member's Bill came before the Seanad (Senate) proposing to allow the Minister for Health to regulate for the sale and distribution of contraceptives.

But the McGee case was the real worry. The extent to which the McGee decision acted as a rallying cry for catholic lay fundamentalists was noted by SPUC president Dr Mary Lucey addressing an anti-abortion gathering, some time after the 1983 abortion referendum. She said: '... we had thought that

19

Ireland would be different - we had the 1861 Anti-Abortion Act. The vast majority of people did not want abortion. It was anathema to 95 per cent of them who were catholic and we thought that our Constitution protected the unborn. We also thought that there were not any abortion referral groups here in Dublin. The decision in the McGee case in 1973 and the simultaneous decision in the Roe v Wade case in North America in the same year brought us to our senses. From that time on we who were interested in unborn human life knew that we must do something.'

The Backlash Begins

In May 1973 just ten months after the High Court rejected Mary McGee's plea against the state seizure of her spermicidal foaming jelly, but just seven months before her Supreme Court appeal was due to be heard, a group called the Irish Family League was founded. Fronted by a woman called Mary Kennedy, newspaper letters from the League in the seventies were also signed by 'Acting-Chairman John O'Reilly.'

But any assessment of the League can be made only with reference to another catholic lay organisation - the Knights of St Columbanus. Later, in 1978, the League was to describe itself as an affiliate group of an organisation also founded that year, the Council of Social Concern, headed by Knight of St Columbanus Nial Darragh and with an accommodation address at the Knights' headquarters in 9 Ely Place, Dublin. And in 1978 John O'Reilly himself formally joined the Knights, many of whose members he had undoubtedly met during his work with the Irish Family League.

At this point it is worth discussing the Knights of St Columbanus, given the role they would play in John O'Reilly's future plans and the role individual Knights, and the Knights as an organisation, would play in the social legislation battle that lay ahead.

The popular view of the organisation is well founded. This sees the Knights as a patriarchal, secretive, catholic, fundamentalist network of influential men who seek to exert power and influence through infiltration of hostile groups and organisations, anonymous lobbying, and the targeting of individuals hostile to their orthodoxy. The Knights also organise pilgrimages to Lourdes, and the Holy Land, and they raise a great deal of money for worthwhile causes such as widows and orphans.

Their fundamental aim is the creation and maintenance of a catholic state for a catholic people and to have enshrined in state legislation the ethos of just one church. A second key aim of the group is the promotion of an employment network for members and for their relatives and friends. A special group within the Knights, the Industrial, Commercial and Professional Panel (ICCP), takes care of their employment interests, looking out for openings for their sons or other relatives, and ensuring that employed Knights will give preference within their particular workplace either to Knights or to those who toe a strict catholic line.

One letter in the author's possession from a Dublin Knight to a member of the Industrial, Commercial and Professional Panel reads:

'Dear X,
Many thanks for your efforts on my behalf for a job.
I enclose cvs for you to pass on to appropriate people.
By the way I am in FF (Fianna Fáil) thirty years. In Brian Lenihan's* (local TD and former Minister) area, but not much use - Albert might do something. (The 'Albert' referred to is the present Taoiseach, but then Finance Minister, Albert Reynolds*.)'

A key Knight involved in business and industry is a former director in the Confederation of Irish Industry, Con Power, who has compiled reports for the Order on various aspects of industrial policy. Mr Power was recently appointed economics advisor to the Taoiseach, Mr Reynolds.

Another key figure is RTE's Assistant Director-General Bobby Gahan who, according to documentation in the possession of the author, was initiated to the Order in 1965 and is now a Knights' trustee. Director of Independent Newspapers, Liam Healy, is also a high ranking Knight and a former trustee.

*There is no evidence whatsoever that either Mr Lenihan or Mr Reynolds acted on or responded to this.

The Knights are encouraged to join social, community, political and other organisations and attempt to direct group policy in a 'Catholic' direction. The degree to which the Knights have succeeded in this can be seen in profiles of those Knights who ran for the top job in 1990, the office of Supreme Knight.

The man elected, Mayo solicitor Charles Kelly, has at various times been a Fine Gael county councillor, chairman of Fine Gael National Council, vice-president of Fine Gael, chairman of Swinford Community Centre, chairman of Swinford GAA club, a founder member of Swinford Credit Union, a marriage advisory counsellor attached to Achonry diocese and the Revenue Sheriff for County Mayo.

Other contenders for executive positions have held similar influential positions both nationally and within their own communities. The occupations of those named in recent years by the Order in internal documents headed 'List of Knights-elect' include: a financial accountant with An Post; an architect with the Office of Public Works; a supervisor with Customs and Excise; a nursing Officer with the Eastern Health Board; the Manager of a Dublin hotel; an auctioneer; a floor manager with RTE; a County Dublin Solicitor; a national school teacher in Dublin; and a senior barman in a Dublin city pub.

This shortlist alone, drawn from lists of hundreds of members around the country, also in the author's possession, shows the wide range of occupations and professions from which the Knights are chosen.

The apex of their power occurred during the first few decades of the new Irish state. In recent years, the Knights have suffered from an ageing and declining membership and intense recruitment difficulties, so intense that consideration has been given to recruiting women members. To date the organisation's hierarchy has resisted all such efforts.

Those who join keep their membership by and large a secret; confidentiality is regarded by the Knights as crucial to their work, as explained in a memo in 1988: '... because members can join and work without fear of penalisation socially or financially, a wider population is available as a catchment area. It can also work more effectively free from media interference and without generating opposition on religious grounds.'

The pledge of the influential ICCP includes a commitment to confidentiality, with the word confidentiality highlighted in bold type. Members are encouraged to join other organisations supportive of their ethos. This amounts to effective infiltration by the Knights of these organisations, without the public being aware of who is actually pulling the strings. Examples include the Society for the Protection of the Unborn Child, Family Solidarity and various catholic interest and pressure groups. The Marian Invalid Fund, and the John Paul II Society, which specialise in pilgrimages to various catholic shrines, are run by the Knights.

Structures Within Knights Of St Columbanus

The Order was founded in Belfast in 1915 by the late Canon James K O'Neill. Its aims, according to the Knights' own literature, were to 'fight discrimination against catholics in all walks of life; to create "leaders of opinion" and to organise catholic gentlemen with a view to such leadership.' By 1926 the Knights had extended their organisation throughout the entire thirty-two counties. Their subsequent infiltration and promotion of key social and cultural organisations was stunning.

In 1929 they promoted and financed the Catholic Boy Scouts. Between 1930 and 1938 they financed the Chair of Catholic Sociology at Maynooth College. In 1931 they set up the nationwide rural education and social network, Muintir na Tíre. By dint of all this great work for the catholic cause they received in 1936 their first invitation to meet the pope in the Vatican. They have been regular visitors ever since.

In 1938 they financed hotel accommodation in Belfast for catholic students and that same year also created and produced the catholic magazine, *Hibernia*. Throughout the 1940s they moved to tighten their grip in every area of Irish public life, gaining representation on various state boards and committees, including the Irish Red Cross, the Royal Hospital for Incurables and the Meath Hospital. In 1948 they founded the Catholic Adoption Society and during the 1950s gained control of the Censorship Board in a bid to 'campaign against evil literature'. In the 1960s they founded the Catholic Communications Centre in Dublin.

The Order is divided into some 100 branches, called councils, into twelve regions, called provincial areas, all administered from national headquarters at Ely Place, in Dublin. A national executive, elected every three years, manages the Order's affairs, led by the Supreme Knight.

The members see themselves as modern crusaders, a Knight in defence of Christ's kingdom on earth. The theme is reflected in their ceremonial garb and language and the elaborate 'robing' and 'disrobing' ceremonies during meetings and other functions analogous to the donning of armour by the mediaeval fighting Knights.

On one level it is the stuff of ridicule and caricature - the idea of middle-aged, middle and lower middle-class men, dressing up, and addressing each other in a manner that can only seem daft to anyone outside the Order. The need to make themselves appear important to each other is paramount. Take for example this setpiece for the installation of primary council officers during the course of Mass as described in the Knights' own literature: 'The DGK (Deputy Grand Knight), preceded by the BB (Banner Bearer), followed by two KCs (Knights of Chapter), enter. All pause at the altar, bow to the cross; the KCs open file to allow the DGK to pass to the lectern/rostrum, preceded by the BB. The DGK turns to the audience, the BB standing behind his left shoulder and addresses them.'

... 'The DGK bows to the congregation; simultaneously the KCs about-turn and take a pace forward; the BB leads the DGK down off the altar/platform where he pauses with his back to the centre of the altar and waits for the BB to pass between the KCs who then close ranks. They all about-turn to face the altar, all bow to the cross, all about-turn and leave the chamber.'

For several years, a debate raged within the Knights as to who should be eligible to wear certain insignia on the cross-shaped robe they wore at meetings and official functions. The final agreement was that the Grand Knight and Deputy Grand Knight could wear a sword on their badges; a Chancellor can wear a skull above his cross; a Secretary can have a feather; an Advocate can have a book; a Warden can have a baton; a Registrar can have a scroll and everyone else is confined to the basic cross.

But if all that seems like so much harmless pomposity, the other work of the Knights is not. In February 1982, for example, a senior member of the Order wrote to 'All Grand Knights' reminding them of the ethical and economic importance of the imminent general election. The Knights were instructed to investigate the views of their local candidates in respect of 'un-christian practices' such as artificial contraception, divorce, abortion and euthanasia. They were also advised to 'target the undesirable candidates for the good of society'.

The chairmen of the various political parties were subsequently written to by the Supreme Knight and asked to state party policy on artificial contraception, divorce, abortion and euthanasia. Every party, bar the Workers' Party, replied.

At a Supreme Council meeting held in Kilkenny the following year, the Supreme Secretary noted:'... (T)he replies from each party were informative and instructive. It will be remembered that Grand Knights and councils were kept informed of these facts during the weeks of electoral activity.'

In fact the two elections in 1982 marked the highpoint of the campaign to target politicians hostile to the Amendment, notably Michael D Higgins in Galway West and Jim Kemmy in Limerick, both of whom lost their seats after a campaign characterised by unprecedented levels of smear and vilification.

In 1984, the Supreme Secretary Diarmuid Moore summarised the Knights' involvement in the campaign at the supreme council meeting in Portlaoise: 'It would be difficult to summarise the work the Order achieved during the Pro-Life Referendum Campaign. It is true to say that most active members, in one way or another, took a large part in the work of winning a 'Yes' vote for Pro-Life. Of particular note is the fact that an Extraordinary General Pro-Life meeting consisting of members of (various tiers of the Knights) took place on Sunday 7 August which attracted a host of newspaper and media folk. The meeting was private, but various inaccurate leaks appeared in the press which showed the interest the Order's work generated during the Campaign. One thing is certain, the prestige brought by the Order to the whole Pro-Life movement was a factor that weighed very heavily in the great success of the Referendum. The record of the Order will rebound to the credit of Catholic Ireland for many years to come.'

In 1983 a similar annual report had noted: 'At both the beginning and end of 1982, the Order found it necessary to protest to RTE for its production of unseemly items.

Fortunately, the Order has been assured that stringent rules were now in operation to avoid such unsuitable transmissions.'

The lobbying of RTE was continuous. Private contact was made with station executives sympathetic to the views of the Knights, while other Knights, purporting to be ordinary, disinterested private citizens, kept up a stream of phone calls and letters to convey the impression of significant public disquiet about particular items.

In 1991, the then Provincial Grand Knight Nial Darragh established in Area 1 a special current affairs team. Darragh outlined that the programme of action for the team would include its monitoring of pressures, campaigns and trends in the media and in society in general. He noted that such a team would alert the Provincial Grant Knight (himself) whenever it saw relevant influences or movements as a result of its monitoring and would determine appropriate action.

The Provincial Grand Knight also noted that when the team is acting on its own initiative it will do so not as part or organ of the Order but under individual's names and private addresses.

One programme subsequently targeted by the Provincial Grant Knight and his current affairs team was produced by a local Dublin radio station specifically for homosexual men and women.

The access the Knights continued to have to the upper echelons of Irish society was frequently boasted about. In October 1983, in a reference to the annual report of the Supreme Secretary stated: 'Following the Supreme Knight's statement of Order policy, advice on this fundamental was asked for and given by the Supreme Knight *even at the highest level in the land* (author's emphasis). This fact is indicative of the Order's standing in society - both lay and ecclesiastically. The Order will have a big part to play during the actual Pro-Life Campaign, that is now, when writing, upon us.'

The Knights' charitable work, which is considerable and well directed, is mixed always with its overriding aim of continuing to have orthodox church teaching enshrined at every level of society. Note the following extracts from the 1988 annual report, detailing the activities of the various Knights' councils throughout the year. (CK refers to a Knights' council - or local Knights's branch.)

CK Five (Derry): Work on establishment of local radio: help in establishing proposed industrial shopping centre.

CK Twenty-eight (Wexford): Constitutional Pro-Life Amendment Referendum: support for Bethany House of Prayer and Knock pilgrimage: planning proper community radio, in association with RTE.

CK Thirty-four (New Ross): Helping local charitable organisations - drug abuse: problems of youth in area: Pro-Life Amendment.

The recent development of community radio throughout the country excited a considerable flurry of activity among the Knights - worried that their influence in RTE would not extend to the new independent stations. Considerable efforts were made, including the holding of information seminars for members, to ensure covert Knights' involvement in the new enterprises.

For an all-male catholic group, the Order's attitude to women is unsurprising. Referred to constantly in their documentation as 'ladies' the Knights' wives are treated with that traditional patronising gallantry that marks covert hostility to the opposite sex. The wives are frequently and fulsomely thanked for such work as cleaning up the Ely House oratory and other menial, subservient tasks. When the Knights set up individual charitable projects in their areas they are encouraged to get 'ladies' committees' involved, presumably to do the leg and donkey work.

In the early 1980s, faced with a declining and ageing membership, a debate took place within the Knights on the possibility of enlisting women members. Unsurprisingly, the first hurdle to be crossed by those anxious for women's involvement was trying to convince their fellow Knights' that women are equal members of the human race. One Knight, Roderick Maguire of Claremorris, County Galway lobbied his fellow Knights thus:

'The following are the reasons put forward by CK 105 for the admission of women to the Order. Since the foundation of the Order a profound change has occurred in the Church and in society with regard to the equal treatment of women. Women are now treated as the equals of men in practically every sphere of life. Women are being admitted in increasing numbers to the professions and are becoming more active in business.

27

'Since women are regarded in the eyes of God as equal to men *and since society in general seems to accept this* (author's emphasis), it is anti-Christian to deny them the right to be members of our Order.'

What is remarkable about the submission from Mr Maguire is the need to assert the equality of women, to let the men know that things have moved on. Also remarkable is the implied acceptance of the fact that many Knights *do not* accept the equality of women. If they did, why then the need for Mr Maguire to spell it out?

The men at the heart of the right-wing drive in Ireland, the men who have campaigned against contraception, abortion, and other measures that allow women to have a public life in this society as opposed to simply a private, domestic life, are partly culled from an organisation in which there exists an element of mysogyny - that includes in its numbers men who do not accept the inherent equality of women in society.

The drive to accept women members was defeated, on the stated grounds that an influx of women would result in the Order being diverted into more and more charitable work and away from its other tasks, ie the infiltration of hostile groups and the guerrilla warfare campaign against the media. In other words the women might become too involved in doing work that actually provides a genuine service to the impoverished and the marginalised in Irish society.

In a 1983 discussion document on female membership the committee on the future development of the Order stated: 'The possibility is mentioned in paragraph 4.9 that a substantial female membership of the Order could lead to an overconcentration in the Order on charitable activities. These activities could be to the detriment of activity on social, economic, and political issues. It could happen in that event that the Order would end up in essence as merely a charitable organisation. This is in no way to denigrate such activities. It just would not be fulfilling the unique lay apostolate role for which the Order was founded and which it has so far carried out so successfully.' The single recommendation from the report was that the Order should not admit women to formal membership.

There is also an element of homophobia in the organisation. An entry in the minutes of the Dublin Area 1 meeting on 22 July 1982 reads: 'Concern was expressed at the increase in the activities of homosexuals and it was suggested that perhaps the Industrial, Commercial and Professional Panel might look into this matter.'

Perhaps the best insight into the working of the Order comes from John O'Reilly himself in a paper written for the Order in 1988. O'Reilly had joined the Order in 1978 but took leave of absence four years later in 1982 to throw himself full-time into the Pro-Life Amendment Campaign (PLAC).

Those four years, as will be shown later, were crucial to the formation of PLAC, with O'Reilly using the facilities and the contacts of the Order to achieve his objective.

In his paper in 1988, a critique of the Order's work, O'Reilly wrote: 'There is much work to do in society today to protect the catholic ethos: we need positive legislation which will help families and the church; we need to amend or oppose unhelpful legislation. We also need to keep our eyes on hospital boards; ethics committees; school boards; parents' groups; the Virgin record store selling condoms to adolescents; family taxation; sex education programmes; trying to keep the right government in power, or at least the one which is the lesser evil.

'Members of the Order should be socially and politically aware and should get themselves on to health boards, hospital boards and any positions of influence for good which exist. The Order should not hesitate to be politically active. What attracted me to the Order initially was the hope that things could be done through it at a quiet and confidential level. The Order has members in many places and walks of life and in positions of influence. *Such a network if well motivated and highly confidential could do wonders quietly without coming out openly as Knights. An organisation or a group is never more powerful than when it influences events without itself being regarded as the initiator.'* (Author's own emphasis.)

O'Reilly then suggests the setting up of new 'special purpose' councils within the Order to take on specific tasks and he concludes: 'These councils should also be empowered to act and lobby on their own provided that they do not do so in the name of the Order, and of course, as is universally normal in the world's intelligence services, if they compromise themselves they would understand at the outset that their actions may be disowned by the Order.'

O'Reilly And The League

But back in the early seventies it was the Irish Family League that served O'Reilly's needs. The stated objectives of the League were to oppose the legalisation of contraception, divorce, abortion and euthanasia, to maintain all articles of the Irish Constitution which 'enshrine Christian values' and to accept amendments to the Constitution only if their intention, they said, mirrored that of Vatican Two, ie 'to penetrate and perfect the temporal order with the spirit of the Gospel ... to infuse a Christian spirit into the mentality, customs and laws and structure of the community.'

The first act of the League was to compile a lengthy booklet on the 'evils' of contraception and distribute it to every TD and Senator. Included in the booklet were the names and home addresses of members and former members of the Family Planning Services Company, plus their occupations, and their involvement in unrelated companies and organisations.

A Mr Francis Crummey for example was described as being 'listed also as director of Prosper Developments. The address of Prosper Developments is 78 Kilbarrack Road, the address of Mr Christopher Morris founder of the Language Freedom Movement. It is also the address of the Irish Humanist Society, the Irish equivalent of the British Humanist Association which played a key role in mobilising support for Britian's notorious abortion legislation.'

The booklet also demonstrated a high level of knowledge of the activities of the international anti-abortion movement with a wide level of sources being quoted to back up the proposition that contraception leads to promiscuity which leads in turn to a demand for abortion.

One factor about O'Reilly, remarked on by his colleagues, is his almost encyclopaedic knowledge of subject matter related to his social legislation crusade. Not alone does he keep a virtual library of press cuttings, books, pamphlets, judicial decisions, etc, but he is also able to recall at will the contents of these when questions are asked or advice sought by his colleagues and followers.

It is also worth noting that two of the international experts quoted in the Irish Family League booklet, would later play a major role in the anti-Abortion Campaign. They were Father Paul Marx, a major Pro-Life campaigner in the USA, who would shortly appear in Ireland armed with his preserved foetus in a bottle to display to school children, and Professor Charles Rice of the Catholic Notre Dame University in Chicago whose advice would be sought almost a decade later on the appropriate wording for the 1983 amendment to the Constitution. And both men would become involved with the Irish anti- abortion lobby at the instigation of Mr John O'Reilly.

With the pamphlet published and distributed to the chosen targets, more direct action was now undertaken by the League. On 19 June 1973, John O'Reilly wrote a letter addressed to the Fertility Guidance Clinic, 10 Merrion Square (later the Irish Family Planning Association) asking for a family planning information booklet and an IUD.

The letter was written in the wake of the High Court decision not to allow Mary McGee's action against the impounding of her contraceptive jelly, but before the Supreme Court case which would be heard later in the year. With the High Court effectively upholding the catholic line on contraception, O'Reilly now saw a way of closing down the fledgling family planning clinics altogether.

He subsequently received a reply telling him about the cost of the insertion of the IUD and enclosing a booklet called *Family Planning for Parents and for Prospective Parents.*

On 26 June, John O'Reilly typed another letter, this time from his Dublin Corporation office, addressed to Family Planning Services and requesting some condoms. But this time he didn't sign the letter himself. Instead he took the letter home and told his then ten-year-old daughter, Deirdre, to sign it. He enclosed a postal order for seventy-five pence and took a carbon copy.

The letter read:
'Dear Sir,
I was told at the Family Planning Clinic that you could supply me with condoms before we try anything else. I enclose seventy-five pence, please let me know if this is not enough.
Yours sincerely,
Deirdre O'Reilly.'

On 14 July, less than three weeks later, Mr O'Reilly's typewriter clattered into action again. This time, an even younger daughter, nine-year-old Eilish, was used as the signatory. The letter was addressed once again to Family

Planning Services Ltd, this time asking for Delfen jellied foam, a spermicide. Nine-year-old Eilish was then told to copy it out, word for word, sign it in Irish (a ploy frequently used by O'Reilly) and give the address of Mr O'Reilly's father in Blackrock, Dublin. This time a postal order for £1.10 was enclosed.

A letter arrived from the company stating that they had no Delfen in stock at that time. Subsequently the spermicide as ordered did arrive.

Five days later, the twelve Durex condoms having duly arrived, John O'Reilly marched down to Pearse Street Garda station, and presented condoms, postal order counterfoil, and carbon copy of the Deirdre O'Reilly letter to Garda Patrick Fennessy. When the Delfen jelly arrived some days later this too was presented to Garda Fennessy.

Garda Fennessy passed the items on to Inspector John Murphy who in turn brought them down to a Dr O'Dwyer, a medical doctor employed by the Department of Health at the Customs House. Dr O'Dwyer 'examined them' and established that the condoms were indeed condoms and that the jelly too was a contraceptive.

Three months later Inspector Murphy interviewed the then chairman of Family Planning Services Ltd, David McConnell and secretary R J Cochrane, pointing out that the sale of condoms was illegal and cautioning them.

Family Planning Services Ltd and the Irish Family Planning Association Ltd were subsequently charged with a range of offences contrary to the state's anti-contraception legislation. The Irish Family Planning Association was charged with distributing the booklet, *Family Planning for Parents and Prospective Parents*, without a permit and with offering and advertising for sale an intra-uterine contraceptive device.

It is interesting that the charges were brought by the Attorney General, Declan Costello, author of Fine Gael's famed *Just Society* document in the 1960s, the man who, as High Court judge in 1992, placed an injunction on the fourteen-year-old pregnant rape victim preventing her from leaving the country to seek an abortion abroad.

The agreement by Costello in 1974 to take action against the clinics on the basis of O'Reilly's complaints was described by the clinic directors as 'exceedingly bizarre'.

The case was heard in February 1974, on the eve of a

Seanad debate on Senator Mary Robinson's latest Family Planning Bill. Under questioning, John O'Reilly acknowledged that his daughters had either written or signed the letters under his instruction. He said that nine-year-old Eilish, who had written looking for Delfen jellied foam could not possibly have known what she was doing. His two young daughters, forced to give evidence in court, acknowledged that they did not understand what their father had asked them to do.

The defence case rested on the fact that there was no evidence of sale, and that the company's documents relating its services stated that they 'do not sell and are not entitled by law to sell' contraceptives. The company instead asked for 'donations' to defray costs. This was disputed by the state who argued that in sending out the jelly and the condoms, there was a clear acceptance of Mr O'Reilly's offer of money.

In the end, District Justice Kearney struck out all the charges, stating that it was clear that the company was not selling contraceptives but accepting donations if the client wished to contribute. He said that the booklet did not advocate unnatural methods of contraception and that the statement in it about the widespread use of the pill around the world as one the most convenient methods of family planning, was a simple statement of fact which could be read in newspapers and magazines every other week.

The case had quite stark parallels with the 1992 rape/abortion case before the High Court. In both cases the full panoply of the state had been used to challenge what in most other western democracies was regarded as a basic civil right; in the O'Reilly case, the right to sell, and give information on, contraception; in the rape case, the right not to carry a pregnancy resulting from an unsolicited act of violence. In both cases the charges brought resulted directly from the actions of John O'Reilly and his associates.

O'Reilly and his support groups would frequently cite the bare detail of the case in their literature, ie that family planning clinics gave contraceptives to children, without ever describing the exploitation of those same children at the hands of their father.

In their comment on the case, Family Planning Services (FPS) declared: 'The Attorney General in 1970 was asked to bring similar charges against the IFPA, but he declined. The complaints on that occasion were made by the same group of people who have been responsible for these charges also. They are a troglodytic, unsavoury, deceitful lot ...

'Such support groups have been responsible for smear campaigns against FPS and the Irish Family Planning Association. They published a booklet *Is Contraception the Answer?* sent to all TDs, councillors and doctors, which was an astonishing collection of casuistic half-truths, sophisms and downright lies. They usually prefer to remain anonymous but have no hesitation in publishing the names and home addresses of all the board members of FPS and the IFPA, presumably hoping they would be run out of their jobs and neighbourhood.'

The anti-contraception lobby was now out in force, beginning to use lobbying techniques which would be perfected years later when the first Family Planning Act was finally steered through the Dáil and later in 1983 when the push was on for the anti-abortion constitutional amendment.

The Genesis Of The Amendment

The idea of a constitutional amendment appeares to have had its first public outing in 1973/1974 in a small leaflet published by John O'Reilly's Irish Family League.

In a short passage referring to the Supreme Court ruling in the McGee case the author(s) wrote: 'The contraceptive issue is a very deep, delicate and divisive one, too important to leave to Oireachtas and Supreme Court. The people should decide the issue themselves by a national referendum. Whether to have or not to have contraception. The law does not have to be changed to conform to the Constitution. We can change the Constitution. *A clause could be inserted defining a citizen as a citizen from the moment of conception and a prohibition on artificial contraception inserted under clause 41*' (Author's own emphasis.) The passage concluded: 'We want a referendum on this issue.'

Ten years later, albeit with slight modifications, John O'Reilly got his wish.

Contraception Law

The day after the O'Reilly court case, on 20 February 1974, the debate on Senator Mary Robinson's Family Planning Bill began in the Seanad. The move by the then Senator to liberalise the contraception laws has long been hailed as revolutionary. Family planning activists at the time thought otherwise, though in fairness to Mary Robinson her bill was very radical for the Ireland of the time.

Irish Times columnist and member of the Irish Family Planning Association, Dr David Nowlan, wrote: 'Senator Robinson herself has come to seem like some sort of revolutionary heroine, leading the battle for human rights through a reactionary Irish parliament. But her bill, if passed, would give Ireland the most conservative and restrictive legislation on contraception in Europe, with the possible exception of Malta, and possibly, Portugal.'

In any event Senator Robinson's bill got nowhere. The day after the debate opened in the Seanad the Minister for Justice Patrick Cooney intervened to say that the Government was going to introduce its own bill within two weeks, thus making the Seanad debate a somewhat academic exercise.

The subsequent introduction of the Fine Gael/Labour Family Planning Bill in July 1974, led to a debate and an outcome that should, almost two decades later, leave those TDs involved in the débacle screaming in embarrassment at the memory.

It is principally remembered for the now Progressive Democrat leader, and then Fianna Fáil TD, Des O'Malley's stirring rhetoric against the evils of 'fornication', and the then Taoiseach Liam Cosgrave's stunning decision to vote against his own bill and drag six of his own TDs with him through the *Níl* (No) lobby.

What was odd about the bill was that it was never actually described as a government bill but rather as a bill that just so happened to be brought in by a member of Government, Justice Minister Patrick Cooney. This little Jesuitical device managed to give the Taoiseach an easy-out when the time came to vote.

Former Taoiseach and then Foreign Affairs Minister Garret FitzGerald describes in his autobiography the valiant efforts made by Cosgrave's ministers to ascertain their leader's thinking on the bill in advance of that vote. 'An episode during this period in government that caused a considerable stir was the defeat in July 1974 of our bill to liberalise the law on contraception. When this matter came before us in the spring of 1974 Liam Cosgrave, who was known for his religious

35

conservatism, stayed silent during the discussion on the terms of the bill. This was not strictly a Government bill but one introduced by the Minister for Justice, Pat Cooney, on his own account, a distinction that I am afraid was far too subtle for many people to grasp. Three times at this meeting Conor Cruise O'Brien endeavoured to extract from the Taoiseach a reaction to the proposed bill, but each time he failed. We left the meeting no wiser about his attitude. The final drafting of the bill and its insertion into the parliamentary calendar took some time, and it was several months later, in July 1974, that the second stage debate was held in the Dáil. Fianna Fáil opposed the bill, in accordance with its consistent policy of supporting the conservative stand-point of the catholic church on such issues, and eventually a vote was called.

'Curiously, despite Liam Cosgrave's silence, even when repeatedly questioned by Conor Cruise O'Brien at the Government meeting months earlier, his stance was not worrying at this stage. Somehow we had managed to convince ourselves that he would support the bill when the time came, the interval since the discussion in Government having insensibly eroded earlier doubts.

'The Chief Whip, the late John Kelly, clearly had no qualms in the matter and was busy persuading the small number of anti-contraception Government TDs that they should vote for it as , according to him, Liam Cosgrave was doing. What we did not realise was that John Kelly had no direct assurance from Liam Cosgrave but was, it seems, relying on an impression of his attitude gleaned from his private office, where the Taoiseach's position had apparently been misunderstood.

'TDs had already begun passing through the lobbies when John discovered his error. Appalled at having misled some conservatively minded deputies into voting for the bill on a false premise, he immediately urged the Taoiseach to vote without delay - for, unaware of John Kelly's activities, Liam Cosgrave had loyally intended to wait until the end before casting his vote so as not to influence other members of his party. Once urged by John, he voted immediately against the bill, and some who had not yet passed through the lobbies decided to follow him. By then, having voted, I was back on the front bench, and, seeing what was happening, I said to Pat Cooney, 'Wouldn't it be funny if he defeated the Government?'

- not realising yet that this in fact was what had happened.'

Despite FitzGerald's hindsight attempts to put a gloss on Cosgrave's actions, the Taoiseach's behaviour was inexcusable on a number of levels, the least of them being that he was grossly disloyal to his colleagues in Government for not having had at least the good manners to inform them of his voting plans.

His behaviour was also sectarian, failing to take into account the non-Catholics in the state whose lives he also legislated for. His stance was finally hypocritical because all that Cooney's restrictive bill sought to do was to regulate for a situation that already existed - to remove the farcical and typically Irish legal anomaly which allowed the free use of contraceptives as long as they were imported from abroad but not sold here - the logical outcome of the McGee case.

The bill's main provision was to legalise the sale through licensed outlets, but to married couples only, another unenforceable Irish solution to an Irish problem but at least heading in the right direction.

The Dáil debate prior to the vote was the usual heady mix on issues of this kind: high farce, stunning hypocrisy and the unapologetic display of pig ignorance. The late Fine Gael TD Oliver J Flanagan, a long time member of the Knights of Columbanus, stated: 'As sure as this bill goes on the statute books it will be the raising of the sluice gates of every kind of immorality with the ultimate result of abortion and all that abortion stands for.'

A Fianna Fáil TD stated: '... bringing in a contraception bill that will ruin the quality of life to which Irish people were used throughout the centuries and for which generations fought and died - and there was no talk of contraception ... if you bring in a bill to make murder legal you won't get me to vote for it.'

Mr Des O'Malley, in his pre-Pauline conversion mode claimed: 'Our duty as a legislature is, so far as we can within the confines of our Constitution, as interpreted for us by the Supreme Court, to deter fornication and promiscuity, to promote public morality and to prevent, insofar as we can - there are, of course, clear limitations on the practicability of that - public immorality.'

Among O'Malley's' suggestions as to how best the McGee ruling could be interpreted was one that proposed that clinics

37

might supply contraceptives to people who were advised by their doctors that they needed them, or that importation for personal use might be permitted.

A note on this matter from a colleague that O'Malley had received when he was Minister for Justice was then produced and read to the Dáil, provoking naturally lots of hilarity from the lads. The note's author, thought to be the late Erskine Childers who was then Health Minister, suggested that 'a reasonable compromise' of what constituted a limited quantity of condoms for personal importation purposes was 'twenty at one time.'

Prior to the debate of course, TDs had received the now familiar missives from John O'Reilly and his Irish Family League. A letter to the national newspapers, signed by O'Reilly and by Mary Kennedy, set out the parameters of their hostility to the bill.

Decrying the 'illegal activities' of the family planning clinics, O'Reilly wrote: 'As a law and order Government we are entitled to demand that you enforce the law, and have a stop put to these activities. We would further ask that you make no change in the existing laws against the wishes of the majority of people who elected you. The consequences could only be inimical to public morality and render the rearing of children still more difficult. Some of these organisations do not differentiate between married and single clients and we have on record that one of them supplied contraceptives to an eleven-year-old child.

'Following the legalisation of contraception and abortion, the next objective of the liberal pressure groups will be to make them a charge on the general tax-payer (the vast majority of whom oppose them). Commerce has a major role to play in this contraception business and its resulting promiscuity, VD and abortion also have business potential. Sex (contraceptive) education in schools is very much the concern of these far-seeing businessmen. Everyone has to plan for the future.'

Poised For The Fray

The mid-1970s were critical years for campaigners on both sides of the contraception divide. Huge momentum was building up for the liberalisation of the contraceptive laws, with a parallel huge momentum to impede that change.

Those opposed to the sale and use of contraceptives could no longer rely on the arguments that had sufficed in earlier years. In one sense the so-called 'contraceptive mentality' had already taken hold. Women had simply realised that fewer babies plus the ability to space their pregnancies opened up opportunities denied to their mothers and grandmothers. It also went some way towards narrowing the gender gap in every other area of private and public life.

Arguments that artificial methods of contraception were morally wrong were simply not going to wash with those women whose lives had been transformed by the gift of fertility control.

John O'Reilly and his associates had to try another tack. The tack adopted was a twin-pronged approach. The first prong was to suggest that artificial methods of contraception were potentially dangerous in themselves and inferior to natural methods on every level.

In February 1975 John O'Reilly, writing as Eoghan O Raghallaigh (though using the same Dalkey address), wrote of the dangers of the intra-uterine device.

In view of what happened with the Dalkon shield IUD many years later, O'Reilly did have a point. However his motivation came from a desire to arouse panic and fear as a campaign tactic rather than from any primary concern for women's health. Mr O'Reilly and his associates had never been too concerned about the effect of multiple pregnancies on women's bodies. What was also remarkable about O'Reilly's letter was the impressive range of medical and other sources he could draw on to back his claims.

The second tack used was not just to make the 'contraception equals eventual abortion' argument but, in order to drive that message home, to hawk around the halls and schoolrooms of the country the QED of that equation - a foetus.

At which point enter Father Paul Marx in the capable hands of Mr John O'Reilly. The reality of abortion in Ireland was being noted prior to Father Marx's arrival in the country and no doubt partly prompted the invitation. Newspaper articles now regularly noted the number of abortions carried out on Irish women in Britain.

In September 1976 British health statistics showed that between 1968 and 1975 10,000 Irish women had had abortions there. The Irish Family Planning Association were now getting two calls a week from women seeking information about abortions abroad.

That same month three significant speaking tours took place around Ireland, all instigated by the Knights of St Columbanus and one directly by John O'Reilly through his wife Treasa O'Reilly.

One of the speakers was Dr Herbert Ratner, described as Associate Professor of Public Health at Loyola University in the United States of America. Ratner had first come to the attention of John O'Reilly when he was quoted by Dungannon catholic priest Father Denis Faul in an *Irish Times* letter to back up his opposition to the contraceptive pill. The quote was subsequently used in the Irish Family League document *Is Contraception the Answer?* in 1973.

Now he was here in person, addressing various small groups throughout the country on the deadliness of the contraceptive pill. Typically, the Knights of St Columnbanus were shy at showing their hand in Dr Ratner's tour, hiding as ever behind hastily formed catholic shelf companies.

In Cork, for example, Dr Ratner spoke to a group called Catholic Witness, whose Cork chairman, according to local newspaper reports, was a well known member of the Knights of Columbanus. Journalists were told at the time that members of Catholic Witness also belonged to the Legion of Mary, The Catholic Boy Scouts, the Ovulation Method Advisory Service, the Family Life Centre and the Catholic Marriage Advisory Council.

At his Cork talk Ratner described the pill as 'chemical warfare against the women of the world', cleverly mimicking the rhetorical style and vocabulary of the women's movement.

At the Kilkenny Clinical Society, describing natural versus 'unnatural' birth control methods the doctor said: 'In Vatican roulette when the woman loses, she at least gains a baby - a baby who very quickly becomes a precious asset. With the pill, the woman plays Russian roulette - when she loses she loses her life.'

Death or an unwanted baby - the great humanitarian choice offered to the country's women by the male doctor and the male shadows responsible for bringing him to the country.

Meanwhile two other like-minded gentlemen were also plying their wares in the country's small towns. This was the double act of Father Paul Marx and Dr Kevin Hume. Dr Hume was a GP from New South Wales, Vice-President of the Responsible Parenthood Association of Sydney. Father Paul Marx was Professor of Sociology in St John's University, Minnesota, Executive Director of the Human Life Centre, and author of works on abortion. Father Marx had paid a brief but infamous visit to Ireland in 1971, gaining notoriety by displaying a preserved foetus in a bottle to school children. Now he and the foetus were back.

Once again the instigators of the Marx/Hume visit remained in the background. This time John O'Reilly used his wife Treasa to front the tour. A letter by Mrs O'Reilly in *The Irish Times* was signed: 'Treasa O Raghallaigh, secretary to the *ad hoc* Committee of Organisers of Father Marx/Dr Hume, 1976, Irish Lecture series.' The address was that of O'Reilly at Dalkey, County Dublin.

The usual 'instant' organisations were also conjured up by O'Reilly as 'hosts' to Hume and Marx, typically fronted by women to disguise the role of the all-male Knights who were orchestrating every single step.

One such group, the Kilkenny Family Life Centre, described itself as 'a group, consisting mostly of wives and mothers who, concerned about the moral and medical dangers of artificial means of contraception, have been promoting natural family planning methods, mostly the Billings method, for the past twelve months.'

The methods used by Marx and endorsed by his Irish promoters nauseated a great many people, with parents particularly incensed at the exposure of their children to such potentially disturbing and upsetting material. One catholic bishop, Dr Browne of Limerick, even walked out of one such talk in protest.

Those opposed to the abortion amendment in 1983 also decried the use by the anti-abortion lobby of pictures of dead foetuses. The use of such methods is a matter of intense debate on both sides of the abortion divide. Should they be accepted in the interests of free speech and liberty or not? Do they play fair?

This argument is most cogently expressed by Harvard Professor of Constitutional Law, Larry Tribe who, in his excellent book published in the late 1980s, *The Clash of Absolutes*, writes: 'In much of the debate over abortion in our society, one side or the other is reduced to ghostly anonymity. Many who can readily envision the concrete humanity of a foetus, who hold its picture high and weep, barely see the woman who carries it and her human plight. To them she becomes an all but invisible abstraction. Many others, who can readily envision the woman and her body, who cry out for her right to control her destiny, barely envision the foetus within that woman and do not imagine as real the life it might have been allowed to lead. For them the life of the foetus becomes an equally invisible abstraction.'

Nonetheless, in Ireland, the reality of the suffering of women who died in childbirth, or died attempting to abort themselves could not easily be hawked around in a glass jar. All that suffering occurred in private. The mere recounting of the tales lacked somewhat the dramatic 'appeal' of the 'preserved' foetus.

1976 also witnessed further attempts to impede the work of the family planning clinics. In October of that year the Society To Outlaw Pornography (STOP) was set up by Nial Darragh, a prominent Knight of Columbanus. Outlawing pornography did seem a laudable aim from either side of the liberal/conservative divide; however, the knights' definition of pornography spanned a very wide brief indeed.

In the 1950s, according to their own official history, they secured control of the then Book Censorship Board, vigorously campaigning against 'evil literature', including the works of Edna O'Brien and John McGahern.

Little wonder then that when in December 1976 (two months after STOP was founded) an anonymous member of the public complained about the Irish Family Planning Association pamphlet, *Family Planning*, the Censorship Board moved with alacrity to ban it on the grounds of indecency and obscenity under the terms of the 1946 Censorship of Publications Act. (The original 1929 Act had specifically banned, in the words of the then Justice Minister Mr Fitzgerald Kenney, 'any free discussion on birth control, which contains, on the one side, its advocacy.') A High Court appeal by the IFPA was upheld. A subsequent appeal to the Supreme Court by the Censorship Board failed.

But one year later, the British feminist magazine, *Spare Rib*, was banned by the Censorship Board presumably because of its 'advocacy' of birth control and other matters anathema to supporters of STOP. The ban on *Spare Rib* and the setting up of STOP coincided with a remarkable period of activity by the Censorship Board.

Between November 1976 (one month after the founding of Darragh's STOP organisation) and March 1977, no fewer than 117 books and three periodicals were banned. There is little doubt that the direct influence of Knight of Columbanus Darragh was a major factor in the heightened activity of the board.

Commenting on the issue in *Hibernia* magazine in March 1977, journalist Brian Trench wrote: 'A letter to the evening papers from Bridget Bermingham, secretary of Parent Concern, one of the several conservative catholic bodies which are most active in lobbying against legalisation of contraception, seemed to indicate privileged information about the issues of *Spare Rib* which had been referred to the Censorship Board. It is more than an outside chance that she herself referred them to the Board.'

In fact Parent Concern would become one of those groups described as 'affiliated' to another Darragh organisation, the Council of Social Concern.

Also in 1977, the Knights scored a major coup in the cultural area. That year, Dublin's Project Arts Centre, staging ground of many *avant garde*, at times controversial, theatrical productions, was refused its customary £4,000 grant from Dublin Corporation. The blame was pinned, according to media reports of the time, on two of the small right wing groupings, the Irish League of Decency and Parent Concern. The League of Decency would also affiliate to Nial Darragh's Council of Social Concern.

Around this time, another man who would play a leading role in the 1983 amendment campaign also came bubbling to the surface - Professor John Bonnar. Professor Bonnar is a Scot whose emigrant father came from Ballybofey in County Donegal. He graduated in medicine from Glasgow University and worked in Oxford until the mid-1970s, when he arrived in

Ireland to take up a position as Trinity College's head of Obstetrics and Gynaecology at the Rotunda maternity hospital, the first catholic holder of the post.

Professor Bonnar is a patron and founder member of a key group in the 1983 amendment campaign, The Responsible Society, launched at the Knights' Dublin headquarters in 1980 and whose secretary and other founder member is - John O'Reilly.

Bonnar's principal crusading objectives were the promotion of natural methods of birth control and the introduction of so-called 'ethics committees' into hospitals, ie committees designed to ensure that the catholic ethos, particularly as applied to gynaecology, obstetrics and birth control, would prevail.

On 2 March 1977, Bonnar was one of three speakers at an Irish Nurses' Organisation (INO) seminar to call for the establishment of ethics committees in *all* hospitals specifically 'to design and monitor hospital policies in contraception, sterilisation and other questions of ethical or moral concern.' He added that there was 'a crying need' for same.

There is little doubt that the policies Bonnar had in mind dovetailed precisely with the ethos and dicta of the catholic church. And just over two years later, in March 1979, the late archbishop of Dublin, John Charles McQuaid, announced the introduction of 'ethical guidelines' for all catholic-run hospitals.

According to the *Irish Catholic* magazine, the archbishop's proposed new code 'envisages the setting up in each hospital of an ethical committee, the members of which are to be chosen by the hospital authority'. The catholic church of course was guaranteed representation on those hospital authorities. It should be noted at this point that the ethos and dicta of the catholic church were already operating very nicely thank you within the country's hospitals; the new ethics code or so called 'Bishop's Contract' simply reinforced what was already in place. (And nothing illustrated just what that 'ethics code' meant in practice better than the case of Sheila Hodgers and her baby. The 'ethics' of her case dictated that she, in agony and riddled with deliberately untreated cancer, should continue her pregnancy for the sake of the foetus until she and her baby both died.)

In October 1977, Professor Bonnar called on the new Fianna

Fáil Health Minister, Charles Haughey, to ensure that natural birth control methods got proper recognition in proposed legislation. And that same month Professor Bonnar described the birth control pill as outdated, claiming that: 'If it came on the market now it would be banned as inefficient and dangerous.'

It is worth noting a reference in Garret FitzGerald's autobiography to the contents of Haughey's eventual family Planning Bill in 1979. Describing a policy paper he had written some time later FitzGerald writes: 'On Church-State relations reference was made to the "powerful campaign of pressure mounted by lay and clerical sources, including organisations like the Knights of St Columbanus, in opposition to the reform of the law on contraception." I referred to the fact that this campaign had been "powerful enough in its impact on Fianna Fáil at any rate to ensure the enshrining of Catholic theology in the form of a reference to "natural family planning."'

Some years earlier John Bonnar had been given a World Health Organisation (WHO) grant to conduct a pilot study on the Billings method of natural birth control. In 1977 Bonnar claimed that his survey to date showed the method was 'embarrassingly successful', with results from India showing a failure rate allegedly far lower than that for any chemical contraceptive.

However, a similar survey published in the British medical journal, *The Lancet*, found otherwise. That survey showed a 22 per cent failure rate for the Billings method. Those surveyed were all clients of the Catholic Marriage Advisory Council, and all well trained in the Billings method.

The Lancet survey was carried out by Professor John Marshall of the Institute of Neurology at the National Hospital in London. Marshall had been a member of the medical council who had advised the pope on his encyclical on contraception and abortion - *Humanae Vitae*. Out of the eighty-four women surveyed by Professor Marshall, twenty-two became pregnant while using the Billings method.

By the end of 1977 the contraception debate was occupying centre stage for quite a number of professional medical bodies as well as for the lay advocates of both sides. In May of that year the Taoiseach Liam Cosgrave, in an interview with the French newspaper *Le Monde*, ruled out any proposal to legalise contraception.

Also in May, Senator Mary Robinson's 1974 Family Planning Bill failed by three votes to get a second reading in the Seanad, but there was evidence from other quarters that the buttress walls against such legislation were continuing to crumble. In April, the Irish Medical Association's annual conference (IMA and IMU joined forces in 1984 to become IMO) backed a motion calling for the free availability of contraceptives including the controversial IUD. The year before, the AGM had failed to pass the same motion. Huge ambivalence still remained. No fewer than fifty doctors present abstained in the vote, with the motion passed by just fourteen votes to ten.

Also in 1977, an indication of the long-term thinking of the anti-contraception/abortion lobby was evident in an article in the Jesuit publication, *Studies*. The author was William Binchy, an eminent barrister and law lecturer specialising in family law. In 1977 he was a research counsellor with the Law Reform Commission and in a powerful position to influence state legal policy and direction.

From 1974 to 1976 he had worked with the Department of Justice as special legal adviser on family law reform. He would later (in 1992) become Regis Professor Elect at Trinity College, Dublin, after holding many prestigious law lectureships abroad. He lectured at the University of Dundee, was Assistant Professor of Law at the University of Ottawa and Visiting Professor at the John Marshall Law School, Chicago. William Binchy has also written widely on family law in journals in Ireland, Britain, Canada and the United States of America.

He would also later become the chief domestic legal expert for John O'Reilly's conservative lobby. Colleagues of Binchy claim it was his writings on the family law area that first brought him to O'Reilly's notice. John O'Reilly had an unparalleled ability to find and accumulate professional people who would not alone provide invaluable advice for his work, but would also give considerable public status to his campaigns. Binchy's 1977 contribution to *Studies* would no doubt have alerted O'Reilly to his propaganda value.

In his article, called 'Marital Privacy and Family Law', Mr Binchy took issue with a previous writer who had argued that the 1973 McGee Supreme Court judgement, decided on a right to privacy basis, could not possibly pave the way for the introduction of abortion. Mr Binchy wrote: 'The concept of marital privacy which McGee has imported into this country from the United States, with little analysis, is of such a pliable nature that it may readily be bent, as has happened in the United States, to accommodate the recognition of the "right" to abortion.'

Mr Binchy also disagreed with the previous writer's assumption that the life of the foetus would be protected through Article 40.3 which guarantees equal rights to Irish citizens. He was not confident that the Supreme Court would accord full citizen rights to the unborn.

In his article William Binchy did not take the next step and argue for a constitutional amendment to Article 40.3 to shore up the rights of the foetus but indicated clearly the steps which the anti-abortion lobby felt needed to be taken to prevent the Supreme Court ever finding in the Constitution a right to abortion.

Binchy made some other observations in his article which are also worth noting. He stated: 'That attitudes regarding abortion are changing rapidly throughout most countries in the world is hardly a matter of controversy. In the United States it was only in the recent past that a small but clamorous band began to agitate for abortion on demand. The changes there have been described as "breathtaking". In Ireland there has so far been little openly-expressed support for abortion. It would, however, seem reasonable to expect that within the next few years attitudes will change somewhat on this subject, as they have done so remarkably on contraception and other matters where religious considerations play a part. To speak there, as Mr O'Reilly (the author of the previous article) does, of "an Irish approach to life which most of its citizens share" and of "the whole ethos of the Irish system" is, it is submitted, to ignore the social realities of Irish life in the seventies, of which, of course, *McGee* is a striking indicium.'

Binchy also noted a 1973 survey on catholic attitudes to abortion in which 74.3 per cent of those polled considered abortion always to be wrong, with 5 per cent tolerating it for social reasons such as the prevention of illegitimacy or in cases of rape. Just 1.3 per cent considered it 'generally right'.

Almost twenty years later a similar survey carried out in the wake of the 1992 case involving the fourteen-year-old rape victim, showed a clear majority in favour of abortion in certain, albeit very limited, circumstances.

In July 1977 Fianna Fáil returned to power with a stunning, and unexpected, twenty seat majority. New Taoiseach Jack Lynch announced his intention to introduce a Family Planning Bill by 1978 under the guidance of new Health Minister Charles J Haughey. Lynch's announcement was the cue for the anti-contraception lobby to gather their troops and prepare for the battle ahead. From 1977 until the passing of the bill in 1979, the Government would be subjected to enormous pressure to either drop their plans altogether or to make access to contraception so restrictive that the bill would scarcely be worth the paper it was printed on.

In January 1978, a notice in *Irish Catholic* magazine stated: 'In an effort to counter unsubtle attacks on our religion, morality and culture, by certain women's organisations and by the lobbies for contraception, divorce and secular schools, a number of socially concerned organisations have formed a confederation, to which they have given the name COSC, Council of Social Concern with a postal address at 8 Ely Place, Dublin 2.'

8 Ely Place is of course the headquarters of the Knights of St Columbanus and the newly appointed chairman of COSC became Nial Darragh, or Nial MacDara as he occasionally styled himself in letters to newspapers. This was a Knightsian habit shared by the man who now emerged as COSC vice-chairman - Mr John O'Reilly, formerly of the Irish Family League. In 1978 O'Reilly had formally joined the Knights.

In fact the founding of COSC can be traced back to pre-1978. Nial Darragh has stated publicly that it was actually formed in 1976 and it was certainly active by 1977. That year they published an unsigned pamphlet, distributed from Ely Place, opposing the Dalkey (multi-denominational) school project and personally attacking some of the project founders.

In 1977, at the Knight's special mass in Dublin's Pro-Cathedral, the then bishop of Kerry, Kevin McNamara, noted the Knights' 'active and corporate endeavour' in 'defence of denominational schooling in Irish society'.

The impressive list of COSC 'affiliates' in 1978 included the League of Decency; the Christian Political Action Movement; Mná na hEireann; Pro Fide; Concerned Doctors Group; Youth Alert; Parent Concern; and the Nazareth Family Movement. COSC (an Irish word which means to forbid or prohibit) also had links with the Catholic Guild of Pharmacists and the Irish Catholic Doctors Guild.

In fact all those groups, many of which had tiny memberships, had as their common base, the involvement and influence of the Knights. Banding them together was a tactic by the Knights both to control their actions and to consolidate combined strength. Some had become disaffiliated by the time the PLAC campaign rolled around in 1983, presumably because of actions even the Knights couldn't condone.

It is worth recalling here the words of John O'Reilly quoted earlier in his critique of the Knights published in 1988. He wrote: 'An organisation or a group is never more powerful than when it influences events without itself being regarded as the initiator.'

The League of Decency had been active for quite a number of years prior to the founding of COSC and its membership included many members of the Knights. Headed by a man called Leslie Quelch it specialised in the plying of politicians with lurid pamphlets on the evils of contraception and other types of 'permissiveness'.

The Christian Political Action Movement was run by a Mrs Manifold and a Mrs Comer in Galway. The two women were first heard of at a public meeting in Galway in 1976 arguing against the setting up of a family planning clinic in the city. In 1977 they published a leaflet naming Labour politician, Michael D Higgins, as being in favour of contraception and urging people not to vote for him. (Clearly not helped by the women's actions, Michael D Higgins failed for the third time in a row to get a seat at the 1977 general election.) During the November 1982 election, they published another leaflet, this time naming the so called 'Pro-Life' candidates and omitting Michael D Higgins. Mr Higgins lost his seat. The only clue to the identity of the leaflet publishers' the initials CPAM and a box number in Dublin. The GPO said the box number didn't exist.

Mná na hEireann, run by Míne Bean Uí Chribín was very much a one-woman show. It was reportedly founded in Cork in 1971 'to counteract the growing women's liberation movement'. In 1982 Míne Bean Uí Chribin said on *The Late Late Show* that the state, through its welfare handouts, encouraged young women to have too many children.

A particularly insidious, and commonly used, tactic of

these groups and of their Knights of Columbanus masters was demonstrated in 1978 when it emerged that letters from the Irish Family League - the organisation founded by John O'Reilly - had been sent to teachers and priests throughout the country calling on them to ensure that Fiona Poole was not elected president of the Irish National Teachers Organisation (INTO). Ms Poole was a member of the Irish Family Planning Association.

In March 1978 the campaign against artificial birth control methods was stepped up, no doubt with an eye to Minister Haughey's proposed Family Planning Bill.

An Irish Medical Association (IMA) committee, headed by John Bonnar, issued a report on the contraceptive pill to an IMA seminar at the association's AGM in Waterford. At the seminar, Mr Arthur Barry (a member of the Irish Catholic Doctors Guild, linked to COSC), consultant gynaecologist at Jervis Street hospital and a former Master at Holles Street, said that prescribing the pill was 'not doctoring at all, it is just butchery.'

In April, the catholic hierarchy issued a joint statement condemning artificial contraception but hinting that the Church would not oppose its introduction as long as it was suitably restrictive - a wish that Mr Haughey would very shortly grant. The statement read: 'The clear teaching of the Church is that it (artificial birth control) is morally wrong and no change in state law can make the use of contraceptives morally right. This teaching is binding on the consciences of Catholics. This is as true in 1978 as it was five years ago. No one can, by passing a law, make what is wrong in itself become right (but) it does not necessarily follow from this that the state is bound to prohibit the distribution and sale of contraceptives.'

In May, Professor Bonnar steamed into action again. Addressing a meeting in Cork organised by the Knights of St Columbanus he urged parents to give their sons and daughters 'protection against those who sought to change the traditional moral values of society'.

That same month Bonnar, along with members of the National Association of the Ovulation Method of Ireland, (yet another organisation with strong links to the Knights, founded in 1976), met with Health Minister Haughey to impress upon him the deadly characteristics of the pill and the IUD and the tremendous success rate of the Billings method.

The representations from the right-wing groups, plus members of the catholic hierarchy had the desired effect. In November, when Haughey finally brought his family planning proposals before the Dáil he freely acknowledged that his bill was designed to restrict, not increase, availability.

Mr Haughey might also have been cautioned by the results of a survey carried out by John O'Reilly's Irish Family League in the minister's own political bailiwick which allegedly showed that 80 per cent of his constituents did not want the free availability of contraceptives.

Introducing the bill for its second reading in the Dáil, the Health Minister said ; 'It is clear to me from my consultations that majority opinion in this country does not favour widespread uncontrolled availability of contraceptives. It emerged clearly that the majority view of those consulted was that any legislation to be introduced should provide for a more restrictive situation in relation to the availability of contraceptives than that which exists by law at present.' (In the wake of the McGee case the legal position, as practised by the voluntary family planning clinics, was that anyone could obtain contraceptives as long as a 'donation' was involved rather than a direct cash purchase.)

Haughey's bill now required that those seeking to purchase any kind of contraceptive, even condoms and spermicides, had to get a prescription from a doctor who in turn had to ensure 'when giving the prescription or authorisation, that the person required the contraceptives for the purpose, bona fide, of family planning or for adequate medical reasons and in appropriate circumstances.'

A special mention in the bill was given to the promotion of natural methods of family planning - a mention which Garret FitzGerald would later attribute to the direct influence of the Knights and others. The minister then drew on the old nationalist card as justification for his restrictive bill, using a now infamous phrase. He said: 'This bill seeks to provide an Irish solution to an Irish problem. I have not regarded it as necessary that we should conform to the position obtaining in any other country.'

The bill was rightly denounced as sectarian, though many commentators were presumably unaware of the extent to which the handiwork of the all-male, all-catholic, secretive

51

band of Knights and their allies had influenced and shaped the final legislation. *Hibernia* magazine's editor John Mulcahy wrote: 'This is a sectarian bill with sectarian intent. It is the product of weak politicians bending in front of the most reactionary element in Irish society today.'

The long-term aims of this 'most reactionary element' were coming into sharper focus though neither politicians nor media picked up the signals at the time.

In October 1978, came yet another signal, the clearest one to date of the ultimate direction of the right-wing lobbyists. On 19 October, in a letter to the *Irish Catholic* by one Eoin O'Máille, the call was made for a constitutional amendment. Mr O'Máille wrote: 'We must press for a precise, Pro-Life amendment to the Constitution where it will be written in that the life of the foetus in the womb is inviolable in all cases, and in all ages, under God, until the end of time.' There was no hint as to the writer's connections. The address given was 24 Plás McLiam, or 24 Fitzwilliam Place.

In November 1978, Monsignor PF Cremin, Professor of Moral Theology and of Canon Law at St Patrick's College, Maynooth, writing in the *Irish Independent* on the proposed family planning bill, described the catholic hierarchy as 'the divinely appointed guardians of morals.'

That may have been the case for the monsignor but at least one group of women failed to agree, nor did they see any reason to wait around for Minister Haughey to introduce his bill. On 27 November, members of the Contraceptive Action Programme (CAP) opened a contraceptive retail shop at 17 Harcourt Road, Dublin, in complete defiance of the law. Within two hours they had sold twenty-five pounds worth of merchandise.

Less than two weeks later the Knights hit back with a booklet called *Gift of Life* which condemned artificial methods of birth control and urged the Government not to legislate in favour of it. Professor John Bonnar's WHO study on natural birth control was extensively quoted and some months later, in March 1979, the booklet was distributed to delegates to the Fianna Fáil Ard Fheis in Dublin.

In early 1979, the Knights were also reportedly organising a signature campaign to petition Pope John Paul II to visit Ireland on the occasion of the centenary of the alleged apparition of the Virgin Mary at Knock in County Mayo.

Several months later, the pope duly arrived complete with messages on the evils of artificial contraception and abortion.

The early months of 1979 also witnessed two more calls for a constitutional amendment to stay the hand of the Supreme Court in relation to contraception and abortion.

In March, a member of Templemore Urban Council, Mr Edward Meagher, in a newspaper letter, called for a referendum to amend the Constitution 'to protect the fundamental right of every human being to be born'. In April a letter on the same lines appeared in the *Irish Catholic*, signed by a C P O'Reilly of Arklow, County Wicklow.

Claiming that any restrictive legislation on contraception could be judged unconstitutional because of the 1973 McGee decision, Mr C P O'Reilly argued that it was first necessary to clear up that constitutional glitch. He wrote: 'And it would be the height of folly to rely on *obiter dicta* from the McGee judgement as offering protection against a Supreme Court judgement in favour of abortion, as such *obiter dicta* do not bind future judges or even the judges who delivered them. The Supreme Court can be checked only by a constitutional amendment bill, which must be approved by referendum.'

By the end of the 1970s the stage was set for a major show-down between conservative and liberal forces. Groups within the general women's movement were forging ahead in their drive to secure contraceptive rights for women. The Well Woman centres had opened in Dublin, providing women with an unrivalled health service including the provision of birth control. The restrictions of the Family Planning Bill were quickly got around. Doctors at the centres provided instant prescriptions and many of the contraceptive devices were available on the premises. Clients did not therefore need to hawk their prescriptions round the city trying to find a chemist whose 'conscience' allowed him/her to fill them.

But most critically, by 1980, the drive for full fertility control, including the right to abortion, was also underway. And underpinning that drive was a belief by the activists that the Constitution contained within it an actual right to abortion.

A February 1980 article in *Hibernia* on the activities of the women's group alerted the right-wing lobby to this new threat. Under the headline 'Feminists Plan Abortion Campaign', journalist, Paddy Prendiville, wrote a speculative piece on the possibility of actually finding a right to abortion within the Constitution - the very scenario William Binchy and others had been musing on and predicting since the 1973 USA Supreme Court Roe v Wade judgement. Here now was proof that their opponents were thinking along similar lines.

Prendiville, who was friendly with a number of the 'right to choose' activists and privy to their thinking wrote: 'Legal speculation on constitutional interpretation of the rights of the woman and foetus centres largely on Article 40 which, it is argued, makes no specific reference to the foetus. It is also pointed out that Article 40.1, providing for equality before the law, states that such equality shall have "due regard to differences of capacity, physical and moral, and of social function," thus allowing for possible distinction between human and foetal rights. Again, the concept of privacy as understood in the American Supreme Court's decisions on abortion and contraception was largely responsible for the 1973 Irish Supreme Court's recognition of the right to use contraceptives. *In theory the privacy concept could pave the way for abortion rights.* (Author's own emphasis.)

'Already a group of determined feminists in Dublin are planning a programme of demands and agitation under the heading of a Woman's Right to Choose. Their demands include the decriminalisation of abortion, open referral for abortions at hospitals and health centres, and the removal of all social and economic discrimination against single mothers. The campaign organisers are presently involved in internal discussion and education but intend to go public in three months time with films and literature on the subject. They also plan to form the Irish section of the International Contraception, Abortion and Sterilisation Campaign.'

Two weeks after the publication of Prendiville's article, the Knights were on the attack. In early March Professor John Bonnar addressed a gathering in the Knights' HQ at Ely House on the topic 'Abortions on Irish Women'. Bonnar warned that well organised pressure groups and international agencies were actively campaigning in Ireland for reforms in contraception, abortion and sterilisation. He said that the protection of unborn life by effective social measures and educational information to change social attitudes was urgently needed and should be a priority of the state.

But if the small pro-choice lobby was finally mustering its

international big guns and going public, their opponents were also harnessing their strengths. The Knights were about to unleash yet another right-wing organisation on to a rather overcrowded market.

In March, the private launch of the Irish section of the British-based Responsible Society had taken place at the Knights' HQ in Ely Place. Among the speakers at the launch on the topic 'The Permissive Society and its Lessons for Ireland' were Professor John Bonnar, Dr Austin Darragh, a brother of Nial Darragh and a specialist in clinical drugs trials, and the late Professor Eamon de Valera, a consultant gynaecologist at the Mater Hospital in Dublin. The Responsible Society was opposed to artificial methods of birth control and abortion and its membership in Britain, and later in Ireland, comprised mainly nurses, doctors and pharmacists.

A pharmacist and prominent member of the Catholic Pharmacists Guild, Bernadette Bonar, now became chairperson of the Responsible Society with the ubiquitous John O'Reilly becoming secretary.

By now, 1980, O'Reilly had founded the Irish Family League, was co-chairman of the Knights'-run COSC, had joined the Knights of St Columbanus itself and was running the latest front group for the activities of like-minded colleagues - chiefly Darragh and Bonar. O'Reilly also edited and largely wrote the Society's newsletter *Response* which monitored the activities of their opponents and rooted out examples of general permissiveness in the country.

O'Reilly's ideas of what constituted permissiveness were very broad indeed and included the activities of the Dublin-based Rape Crisis Centre and a group called SPOD, which provided an advisory service for disabled people on their sexual problems.

In one edition of *Response* O'Reilly wrote: 'SPOD and the Dublin Rape Crisis Centre are examples of how ultra-permissive forces can fasten on to what appears to be a compassionate or charitable cause.' SPOD was condemned for its 'promotion of mechanical activity for its own sake ... learning the techniques of sex and masturbation in an amoral context.'

In 1981 the Responsible Society fought against the renewal of the Government grant to the Rape Crisis Centre. The newsletter commented: 'It is our belief that in funding the

Rape Crisis Centre, the state is funding and lending respectability to promoters of abortion, even though the amount is small and it cannot be proved as such that the Rape Crisis Centre is in anyway connected with abortion or abortion referral.' After a long fight, the grant was paid to the centre at the same rate as for 1980 which was well below the expectations of the centre and thus represented a victory of sorts.

In August, the group heralded by *Hibernia* was launched in the Junior Common Room in Trinity College, Dublin. Calling itself the Woman's Right to Choose Group, its stated aim was to fight for the decriminalisation of abortion and for full access to abortion facilities. One month later, the first pregnancy counselling and abortion referral centre, the Irish Pregnancy Counselling Centre (IPCC), was opened at 3 Belvedere Place, Dublin. By the time it went public that month, 250 women had already received counselling on the abortion option.

The Knights' response, through Nial Darragh, was to send a telegram to the Taoiseach urging him to move against the referral agencies. In August Darragh had written to the *Irish Catholic* magazine urging people to phone and write to top Fianna Fáil TDs, stating that they did not want contraceptives sold in their area. Signs of even more frenzied activity on the anti-abortion/contraception front became evident within weeks of the opening of the counselling/referral centre.

In September two critical anti-abortion conferences took place in Dublin, one of which, at Trinity College, is frequently cited in the media as the genesis of the Pro-Life Amendment Campaign. Yet the history of the anti-contraception/abortion lobby shows that its real origins go back quite some years before 1980.

That September Professor John Bonnar organised a conference at Trinity College, Dublin under the auspices of the Dutch-based World Federation of Doctors who Respect Human Life. The federation is committed to defending 'the sanctity of the human person from conception to death'.

About 200 doctors attended, including Dublin gynaecologist, Dr Julia Vaughan, soon to emerge as the main frontperson for the Pro-Life Amendment Campaign. Vaughan, a former nun, was a highly respected gynaecologist with a practice at the catholic Mount Carmel private hospital in Dublin. O'Reilly's colleagues have claimed that he saw in

Vaughan an ideal frontperson for the kind of campaign he was now planning. Her major attraction was that she was a woman and would offset negative reaction to the preponderance of male activists, but also her reputation as a gynaecologist would help bring other eminent gynaecologists on side.

The dominant theme of the Trinity College conference was abortion, with delegates told how pressure from groups such as the International Planned Parenthood Federation was influencing abortion laws world-wide. Members of the Catholic Doctors Guild attended the conference, some of whom had already discussed among themselves the idea of a constitutional amendment to outlaw abortion.

The Catholic Doctors Guild had strong links with the Knights-controlled Council of Social Concern and included in its membership Professor John Bonnar, Dr Julia Vaughan, Professor Eamon de Valera and Dr Richard Wade. Dr Wade's name appears on internal Knight's documentation in the author's possession.

The guild was another useful front organisation for the Knights. Its beauty was the respectability which its members would lend to the abortion amendment campaign. Its chairman, Dr Dominic O'Doherty, allowed his address to be used in the early literature for the Pro-Life Amendment Campaign while its president Dr Arthur Barry and Professor de Valera became founding patrons of the campaign. Early histories of the campaign focused almost exclusively on the activities of the doctors, while the real instigators and activists like O'Reilly and others hid unnoticed in the shadows.

Some of the more fervent anti-abortionists at the Trinity conference staged an auxiliary conference of anti-abortion pressure groups at Carysfort Teacher Training College in Blackrock, County Dublin. The groups attending that conference included the Responsible Society, the British Society for the Protection of Unborn Children (SPUC), and several of the doctors from the Trinity conference. In SPUC, John O'Reilly found another organisation within which to operate, becoming a council member at an early stage.

Also in attendance at the Carysfort conference was Father Paul Marx, the anti-abortion priest brought over by John O'Reilly in the seventies to lecture on the evils of abortion.

One of the key speakers at the Carysfort Conference was Dr Peggy Norris, representing the 'International Pro-Life Service'.

Dr Norris warned that Ireland, could soon have abortion on demand and, demonstrating a surprising knowledge of pro-choice activity in Ireland, noted the forthcoming international seminar on the right to choose question. Dr Norris warned that the pro-choice advocates would not go away until there were abortion clinics in Ireland or until 'sufficient Pro-Life forces have been mustered to defeat them'.

In October, the conference noted by Dr Norris duly took place in Trinity College. A public meeting on 'Abortion - an International Issue' marked the opening of the International Contraception, Abortion and Sterilisation Campaign conference. The campaign had been founded in 1978 by Dutch and British feminists in response to the growing world-wide anti-abortion campaign.

The two sides were now poised for the fray...

Steps To A Referendum

The two anti-abortion conferences had not come about by accident. Both were part of a grand plan hatching in the mind of John O'Reilly. Contemporary accounts of the setting up of what would become the Pro-Life Amendment Campaign traced its origins to various informal and formal meetings of doctors, mainly gynaecologists. It suited John O'Reilly that this should be the public perception but it was quite far from the truth.

In early 1980 the Council of Social Concern (of which Nial Darragh was chairman and John O'Reilly vice-chairman) discussed once again the idea of an amendment to the Constitution, to ban abortion. This idea, as seen earlier, had been discussed for several years. The advent of the right to choose group plus the abortion referral centres added a sense of urgency to the discussions. O'Reilly now felt it was time to act.

According to one account of the amendment campaign, *The Second Partitioning of Ireland*, written as a doctoral thesis by Queen's University Belfast tutor, Tom Hesketh (under the direction of Professor Cornelius O'Leary who would later become PLAC vice-chairman), legal advice was sought by COSC on the amendment proposal. The Knights of Columbanus were then asked by John O'Reilly to coordinate the operation and contact other groups.

According to Hesketh, who was given access by John O'Reilly to a considerable amount of PLAC documentation, the Knights refused to be the coordinators of the amendment campaign on the grounds that such an amendment might be lumped in by the Government with an amendment to remove the constitutional ban on divorce.

Hesketh may not have been fully aware of the degree of Knights infiltration within the existing right-wing groups, including COSC. Whether the knights became formally involved or not was largely irrelevant because their members as well as their *modus operandi* were all over this fledgling campaign from the beginning.

At any rate, a key tactic of the Knights was never to publicly declare their hand in any campaign but to pull the strings nonetheless. Documentary evidence proves beyond doubt the major role played by the group in the campaign.

There is no way that an organisation openly and publicly fronted by the suspect Order would have gained the political access PLAC finally did gain.

In July 1980 John O'Reilly prepared a formal circular letter, proposing the amendment idea, for distribution to like-minded groups. In September the Irish Catholic Doctors' Guild was contacted. According to O'Reilly in a lecture he delivered after the 1983 referendum, the Irish Catholic Doctors' Guild had also been thinking about a so called 'Pro-Life' amendment. This was hardly surprising given that one of its key members was Professor John Bonnar, a close associate of John O'Reilly's through their membership of the Responsible Society. Dr Richard Wade, a Knight and another member of the Responsible Society also belonged to the guild. The guild was an effective affiliate of O'Reilly's and Darragh's Council of Social Concern (COSC).

William Binchy would also join O'Reilly around this time, and become one of PLAC's many legal advisors. Some time before the official founding of PLAC Binchy had delivered a lecture at the Coombe Hospital which gave a legal perspective to the central theme of the lecture series - ethical issues in reproductive medicine. The lecture detailed the history of abortion laws in the USA and the history of birth control laws in Ireland. Binchy pondered how one could legally protect the right to life of the foetus. He too mooted the idea of the constitutional amendment while expressing some concern about the divisiveness and emotiveness of a referendum campaign.

More intriguingly, Binchy debated the pros and cons of seeking injunctions against women seeking abortions abroad, though this was in the context of the law as it stood at the time and not as the result of a future amendment. Acknowledging that such injunctions would be met 'with a barrage of criticism by those who favour abortion on the basis that it amounts to an inhumane attempt to persecute and make criminals of girls who have been driven by an uncaring society into taking this step as a last resort', Binchy nonetheless continued in *Ethical Issues in Reproductive Medicine: A Legal Perspective*:

'Yet the philosophy on which these criticisms would be based can itself be challenged. If these criticisms have any validity, we should not only make it lawful to go to England to have an abortion: we should also have to make abortion lawful here. Yet the public policy of the state - and the virtual moral consensus in our society - opposes the legalisation of abortion. The view is taken that the life of the foetus must be protected, however sympathetic one may feel towards the plight of the child's mother who is tempted to terminate its life. If we were to allow sympathy for the woman to stop us from regarding abortion as criminal when performed on an Irish girl in England, why should that sympathy stop at our shorelines? Similarly, if we regard abortion as wrong when performed here, why should it become right when performed fifty miles away?

'If the law were to make it an offence to have an abortion in England, there would be a massive controversy: the proponents of the legislation would be vilified and branded as persecutors and hypocrites. It would require some strength of character for our politicians to withstand this barrage of criticism, but a strong argument can be made that our law should give such effect as it can to the principle that unborn life is entitled to be protected.'

Binchy's remarks are particularly fascinating given that, in the wake of the 1992 case in which a fourteen-year-old rape victim was banned from seeking an abortion abroad, Binchy and his colleagues denied that it had ever been their intention to prevent women from going to England for abortions.

By January 1981 O'Reilly had received positive responses from twelve organisations and was confident of five more. Plans were now made for a founding conference. Dublin solicitor and Responsible Society member Denis Barror along with Queen's University Professor Cornelius O'Leary would deliver papers on the legal and political aspects of the proposed amendment. Professor O'Leary was a frequent letter writer on moral issues to the newspapers. This had clearly not escaped O'Reilly's notice.

John O'Reilly then drew up a campaign blueprint, drawing heavily on the idea of a nationwide signature campaign which would force the Government to concede a referendum. O'Reilly also wanted to establish a nationwide committee network to fundraise and canvass and which would then be left intact for the next battle, possibly divorce. (This idea was realised by O'Reilly in 1984 with the setting up of Family Solidarity, the organisation which provided the ground troops for the 1986 anti-divorce campaign.)

The founding conference was held on 24 January 1981, in Mount Carmel Hospital, Dublin where Dr Julia Vaughan had her practice. The following groups were represented: Congress of Catholic Secondary School Parents' Association; Irish Catholic Doctors' Guild; Council of Social Concern; Guild of Catholic Nurses; Guild of Catholic Pharmacists; Catholic Young Men's Society; St Thomas More Society; Responsible Society; Society for the Protection of Unborn Children; Irish Pro-Life Movement; National Association of the Ovulation Method; St Joseph's Young Priests' Society; and the Christian Brothers School Parents' Federation. The Irish Nurses' Organisation (INO), Muintir na Tíre, and Pax Christi Christian Life Communities all sent messages of support.

A newly formed Irish offshoot of the British based Lawyers for the Defence of the Unborn later affiliated. Leading lights included William Binchy and Senior Counsel Dermot Kinlen. Denis Barror also introduced the group to Senior Counsel John Blayney who would later play a key role in the campaign.

The delegates were addressed by COSC chairman and Knight of St Columbanus Nial Darragh and asked for their active support for a 'Pro-Life' Amendment Campaign. One week later a similar meeting was held, also at Mount Carmel, with the delegates addressed this time by Professor Cornelius O'Leary.

An executive committee was then selected with Dr Julia Vaughan becoming chairperson of what was now known as the Pro-Life Amendment Campaign (PLAC). Michael Shortall of the Catholic Young Men's Society was elected secretary and Denis Barror of the Responsible Society became treasurer. Professor O'Leary became vice chairman.

Another crucial recruit at this point was Brendan Shortall, a public relations specialist, who was invited to become involved by his brother, Michael Shortall, now secretary of PLAC. Shortall had worked for a number of years with a commercial PR company, Public Relations Practitioners (PRP). He left PRP to set up his own PR consultancy, run from his Sutton, Dublin home and specialising in the application of commercial PR techniques to social and political issues. One commission, for example, was the promotion of parents' councils in catholic secondary schools.

PLAC was formally launched with a press conference on 27 April, 1981. The press release listed a number of prestigious medical patrons, including Professor Bonnar and Professor Eamon de Valera. The other patrons were the top gynaecologists and obstetricians in the main teaching centres around the country. No other individuals or affiliated groups were mentioned.

A draft amendment was unveiled at the launch which left few in any doubt about the absoluteness of the PLAC position. Some also noted the implicit secondary importance their amendment wording attached to the woman's life. The draft had been drawn up by Senior Counsel, John Blayney, who later went on to become a Judge to the High Court. The draft amendment read: 'The State recognises the absolute right to life of every unborn child from conception and accordingly guarantees to respect and protect such right by law.'

In fairness to Blayney, according to Hesketh, the word 'absolute' was inserted by fellow lawyer Frank Ryan and was recognised as being legally questionable by others in PLAC. It was not, however, changed. Such a wording, had it been carried, would deny all rights to the woman even in cases where her life was threatened by continuing pregnancy. That such a wording should emanate from a group sponsored by practising gynaecologists was deeply disturbing. It did not, however, raise alarm bells in the minds of the leaders of the two largest political parties.

In fact for some in the group, notably John O'Reilly and his two organisations, COSC and the Responsible Society, the wording didn't go far enough. They wanted the word 'fertilisation' inserted as opposed to 'conception.' O'Reilly, along with John Bonnar and others, had an eye to an amendment that would allow for the banning of the IUD and possibly certain forms of the pill. As the IUD can work after fertilisation has taken place, an amendment giving foetal rights from fertilisation could possibly include a probihition of IUDs.

Early in 1982 O'Reilly would write in the Responsible Society newsletter: 'We must ensure that it is the right kind of amendment which will protect human life from conception (fertilisation). With the newer and coming advances in abortion technology which act at the very stages around fertilisation and implantation, it is most important to have the beginning of life defined and protected. Else we end up in the same position as the IUD under the present law and despite our Pro-Life amendment the way would still be open for abortion by prostaglandins, menstrual extraction etc. We will have to ensure that the Amendment is watertight *and allows no exceptions* (Author's emphasis). Similarly it must be certain that the amendment will not prohibit treatment for cervical cancer and ectopic pregnancies which are not abortions at all though indirectly and unintentionally they lead to the death of unborn babies. Whatever amendment is produced will have to be looked at to see that it is watertight enough and sufficiently comprehensive.'

Note O'Reilly's reference to ectopic pregnancy and cervical (or uterine) cancer - the only two exceptions he (and the catholic church) make to the anti-abortion ban.

The general belief that the church allows for abortion in all cases when a woman's physical life is threatened is simply not the case. Even in those two exceptions, the church has consistently stated that it is not making a choice between mother and child, but between the certain death of both and the survival of the woman, ie only when both are certain to die if the pregnancy continues, but more crucially *during* the term of the pregnancy, can abortions be sanctioned.

In no case does the catholic church assert a superior right to life to the woman despite the common misconception that it does. In other words, in all cases where the death of the woman is not certain, ie a chronic heart condition made worse, but not fatally so in the short term, by pregnancy, abortion is not sanctioned by the church. This was the dilemma faced by doctors in the Sheila Hodgers' case detailed above. Aborting a foetus to allow for medical procedures for non-uterine cancer is simply not condoned by the catholic church.

In Sheila Hodgers' case both mother and child did die but as the child's death was not certain, and Sheila Hodgers did not actually die while pregnant, the hospital did fully conform to catholic church teaching and the ethos of John O'Reilly and many of his colleagues.

It is worth quoting again from Uta Ranke-Heinemann's book *Eunuchs for Heaven*. While speaking specifically about the German catholic experience, her observations are equally valid for any catholic country. She writes: 'Until quite recently, women giving birth in Catholic hospitals could be deprived of urgent medical assistance and their lives placed in jeopardy if the hospital authorities adhered to official Catholic doctrine,

64

which holds that it is more important to baptise a moribund child than to let it die unbaptised and save its mother's life. They are still at risk where the official line continues to hold sway, for this macabre chapter is far from closed.'

'As far as Germany is concerned, the danger has somewhat diminished since 7 May 1976, when the German bishops resolved to "respect" (but not endorse) "conscientious medical decisions in hopeless situations where a choice must be made between losing the lives of both the woman and the unborn child and losing one life only". In plain language, if woman and foetus were both dying, the bishops would acquiesce in the doctor's decision to save the life of the woman by sacrificing that of the foetus. In even plainer language: the doctor was permitted to save the woman by aborting her, only if she *and* the foetus would otherwise die, not if it was a simple choice between the woman and the foetus. This, however, was merely a concession to doctors who deviated from true Catholic doctrine.

'Commenting on the bishops' ruling on 31 May 1978, the Jesuit periodical *Orientierung* as cited in *Eunuchs For Heaven* wrote: "Respect does not necessarily connote approval, and no one, on the basis of this grave declaration, which betokens respect for conscientious personal decisions taken in hopeless situations, should underestimate the courage, self-sacrifice and heroism of those women who die rather than betray their consciences." In other words, the only good mother in such cases is a dead mother, for only the woman prepared to die with her foetus can be said to have a clear conscience. Bernhard Haring, the Catholic moral theologian, wrote in 1985: "I shall not here deal in detail with the termination of pregnancy, whose sole (objective) purpose and sole (subjective) intention consist in saving the woman's life when there is no further chance of saving the life of the foetus. We must beware in such (very exceptional) cases of breeding guilt complexes, which often lead, as we all know, to extremely disturbed human relationships and to a distorted image of God".

'So a woman is entitled to live on without guilt complexes and disturbed human relationships if her life has been saved by the abortion of a foetus which was past saving in any case.

'The decision is not hers, however. The German bishops consulted no expectant mothers. Their letter was addressed to doctors and acknowledged *their* right to be guided by conscience. The women concerned were merely transferred from one sphere of alien-jurisdiction to another. The Gods in black had ceded their right of life-or-death decision to the gods in white or green'.

Thanks to (the German bishops) ... 'we have now reached the stage in Germany where only one life must be sacrificed instead of two provided the obstretician's conscience so decides. The Church's official doctrine, which remains unrevoked and in force, takes a different view, and many other countries have yet to sidestep the Vatican's rulings. Furthermore, the German bishops' declaration is nowhere near as favourable to the woman as it has been painted. They leave it to the doctor's absolute discretion which of the two lives he may legitimately save, given that both would otherwise be past saving. According to their declaration, he can rest assured of the same episcopal respect if he decides to save the child's life and kill the woman. Fortunately for expectant mothers, they have since been spared the dire consequences of such an appalling episcopal ethic by doctors' consciences and advances in medicine.

'... (but) progress in medicine has merely made it easier to survive the science of theology - not that this will breathe new life into the many women whom theologians have killed over the centuries. Today's life-saving medical exercise of conscience would not have accorded with "the most steadfast will of Our Most Sacred Lord" as interpreted by the Vatican on 1 August 1886. These were the words it employed when confirming a decision handed down on 28 May 1884. Cardinal Caverot of Lyon had questioned whether it was legitimate to perform a craniotomy (cutting or crushing the foetal head to facilitate delivery) when mother and child would both die in default of such an operation, but when the woman alone could be saved by it. Rome's negative response of 1884 was extended on 14 August 1889 to cover "any surgical operation that directly kills the foetus or the pregnant mother". On 24 July 1895, a physician asked Rome if, in view of the above rulings, he was entitled to "save the mother from certain and imminent death by artificially delivering a not yet viable foetus using methods and operations that did not kill the foetus but endeavoured to deliver it alive, whereafter, being immature, it expired. The response was another negative and this decision was repeated in 1898. In condemning abortion on medical grounds in 1930, the encyclical *Casti connubii* declared: "What could ever be a sufficient reason for excusing in any way the direct murder of the innocent? ... Those show themselves unworthy of the noble medical profession who encompass the death of one or the other, through a pretence at practising medicine or through motives of misguided pity."'

So, in April 1982 as the PLAC team prepared to meet with the Taoiseach and party leaders, the stated belief of John O'Reilly, the person who had brought them to this point, was: in situations where a woman's life was threatened by medical conditions other than the two sanctioned by the catholic church a termination of pregnancy cannot be condoned.

PLAC wasted no time. Just three days after its formal launch, a delegation was inside Government Buildings lobbying the then Taoiseach, Charles J Haughey, for a referendum to amend the Constitution. A meeting was also held with Fine Gael leader, Garret FitzGerald. The meetings were arranged by Brendan Shortall and positive responses were promptly received. Shortall's letter gave no historic account of the genesis of the campaign, or who was involved behind the scenes; he simply stated that the country's top gynaecologists and obstetricians were rather concerned about the possible threat of abortion and would like to discuss this with the party leaders.

The delegations were mainly led by Julia Vaughan while the rest of the mix was changed to suit the 'taste' of the political party leader. Thus, while Julia Vaughan led the discussion in the meeting with Charles Haughey, Professor Eamon de Valera held the floor at the Garret FitzGerald meeting. It was felt that Mr Haughey might not take too kindly to being lectured on the Constitution by its author's son. FitzGerald, however, it was decided, would adopt a very deferential attitude to the professor.

Loretto Browne of SPUC was also on the PLAC delegation along with lawyers Frank Ryan and Denis Barror. Brendan Shortall attended every meeting. As the acceptable face of PLAC, the combination was perfect. Not a Knight in sight. At least as far as one was aware. None of the loonier elements of the catholic lay groups were allowed stick their heads over the parapets at this point either.

The timing of the meetings was perfect. The Haughey minority Government was barely clinging to power. A general election was being widely predicted. The possibility of playing one side off against the other on such an intensely emotional issue was tantalisingly present and would later define the referendum campaign.

Garret FitzGerald was also particularly vulnerable on the abortion issue owing to a publicly damaging internal party row on that very issue. Some weeks before his meeting the PLAC delegation, a young Fine Gael member, Maria Stack, had apparently spoken out in favour of abortion. She later said she was misquoted and that she was in favour of abortion only when a woman's life was at risk. Nonetheless, there was fury within the party at her remarks, with front bench TD, Paddy Harte declaring that abortion was not even a topic fit for discussion. In addition, said Mr Harte, anyone who supported abortion should be expelled from the party.

FitzGerald moved quickly to defuse the row, stating, on 6 April, that Fine Gael was unalterably opposed to abortion. He added that at the 1980 Young Fine Gael conference, they had declared their recognition of the right to life of the foetus 'from the moment of conception'. Even the party's spokesperson on Women's Affairs, Gemma Hussey, added her tuppence worth, telling *The Irish Times* that she was opposed to abortion under all circumstances, seeing it as a matter of human life, and not women's rights.

It is worth noting that FitzGerald, in his autobiography, *All In A Life*, devotes just eight pages to the 1983 amendment campaign. Compare this with the 112 pages devoted to the New Ireland Forum and the Anglo-Irish Agreement. FitzGerald recalls that the PLAC delegation told him that in the light of the 1973 USA Supreme Court judgement in the Roe v Wade case (which had effectively declared anti-abortion legislation unconstitutional), steps should now be taken by the Irish Government to ensure that no such decision would ever be taken by the Supreme Court here.

FitzGerald immediately, and apparently without question or equivocation, agreed to the PLAC demand for support for such a move. One member present at the meeting described his attitude as 'grovelling'. FitzGerald later wrote: 'It seemed highly improbable that our court would in any conceivable future make such a decision, but, influenced in part by my personal antipathy to abortion - one of the few issues on which there was a united view - I agreed to support an amendment to the Constitution that would limit the court's functions in this matter. A month later I included a commitment to this effect in the Fine Gael election programme.'

It seems extraordinary that a man of FitzGerald's intelligence, with his pluralist outlook, his much-vaunted academic interest in theology and other religions, his antipathy to the sectarian nature of much of the state's laws and constitutional provisions, should have bowed the knee so quickly and so unthinkingly to those people. The most cursory enquiries about the attitude of non-catholic churches to abortion would have demonstrated the lack of absoluteness in their positions, with a greater weighting accorded to both the life and the liberty of the woman.

Hesketh's book reveals that FitzGerald's account of the first PLAC meeting may have had one significant gap. SPUC activist, Loretto Browne, revealed in 1982 that FitzGerald even undertook to introduce a draft Pro-Life amendment as a Private Member's Bill if the threatened impending general election didn't occur. The actual PLAC records of the meeting did not refer to this alleged commitment. However the author has learned from another member of the PLAC delegation that FitzGerald did indeed make this commitment.

Ironically, in view of his later stance on the issue, the then Taoiseach Charles Haughey was not as clearcut in his support of the amendment as FitzGerald had been when he met PLAC. Haughey agreed in principle to an amendment but asked for more time to consider the matter. On 13 May 1981, however, at a further meeting with the PLAC delegation, all equivocation had gone. In a letter dated 14 May, Haughey wrote to PLAC: 'Further to our discussion on 13 May, 1981, I wish to convey to you, on behalf of the Government, a solemn assurance that an appropriate constitutional amendment to give effect to that position will be brought forward as soon as circumstances permit. We are at present examining the form such an amendment will take so as to ensure that it will be fully constitutionally and legally effective.'

On 12 May the delegation met with the then Labour Party leader, the late Frank Cluskey, and Labour TD, Barry Desmond. The two men merely agreed to consider the need for a referendum, but their June 1981 election manifesto never mentioned the amendment demand.

In June 1981 John O'Reilly and Nial Darragh wrote to the PLAC executive outlining ideas for the next stage of the campaign. Tensions had arisen between what could loosely be termed the fundamentalist wing of the PLAC group, notably O'Reilly, Darragh and the SPUC activists, who wanted a no-holds-barred campaign with plenty of publicity and controversy, and the more moderate wing under Julia Vaughan who wanted to play it softly-softly and not turn it into a political football if it could be avoided.

The O'Reilly/Darragh letter was an attempt to steer the campaign in a more directly confrontational direction. O'Reilly/Darragh feared that an anti-amendment campaign would soon emerge and immediately steps needed to be taken to counteract that. The letter stated: '... (I)t would appear that PLAC fails to realise that the international abortion movement will launch an intensive brain-washing campaign here as soon as the Referendum is definite - if not before ... If a date next April is named, we could expect the counter-campaign to mount before Christmas, less than six months from now ... We have been given a respite of some months. Let us use it fully to get our strategy right, our funds in order and to build up our human resources. The international abortion movement is more powerful than even well-informed people realise, often working through international agencies held in great respect ... The strategy, no doubt, would be to spread confusion by arguing for abortion in cases of rape, incest, alleged "life and death" situations, and in the case of foetal abnormality. As usual, the pro-abortion campaign will be highly emotive and libertarian. To counter it, emotion will have to be made to serve the unborn and their sense of human rights and justice invoked.'

Mr O'Reilly's viewpoint on such 'emotive' issues as pregnancies that arise out of rape, intercourse between father and daughter, or what he terms 'alleged life and death situations' is worth noting. The humanity directed at the foetus is palpably absent when the woman's life and liberty is considered. One could wonder whether O'Reilly and his colleagues actually believed that the woman shared even equal humanity to the foetus. Recall how the Knights had to be told by a member of their Order that a woman *was* considered equal in all respects to a man during the debate on the admission of women members.

It is also worth noting that the anti-abortion lobby are opposed even to the abortion of an encephalic foetus, literally a foetus with no brain but rather a brain stem - and utterly incapable of surviving outside the womb for more than a short time. The anti-abortion lobby would rather that a woman, knowing from early on in her pregnancy of the foetus' condition, should continue that pregnancy to term and give birth to a baby that would die within days, sometimes seconds. The emotional impact on such a woman is unimaginable.

On how the anti-amendment campaign should be countered, O'Reilly stated: 'We need money for literature, radio and TV coverage, newspaper promotion as well as quantities of coloured literature on pre-birth life ... All this will require sums of money, say a bare minimum of £100,000, doing it on a shoestring; up to a high of £600,000.' In his memo O'Reilly also insisted on an amendment wording which protected life from the moment of fertilisation. He suggested enlisting the aid of doctors and lawyers from abroad conversant in Pro-Life legalities.

As early as July of 1981 O'Reilly had enlisted the help of one such expert - Professor Charles E Rice of the University of Notre Dame in Indiana, a hot-bed of Pro-Life radicalism. On 21 July Rice wrote to O'Reilly saying: 'Enclosed is the text of the Human Life Bill approved by the Senate Judiciary sub-committee and some related material. I am sending it to you because it may suggest a way out of the conception/fertilisation problem ... I hope this will be helpful. Please let me know if there is anything further I can provide.' (Later it was assurances from Rice to O'Reilly about the acceptability of the final Fianna Fáil amendment wording that led to O'Reilly and his group giving it the go-ahead.)

One other man in touch with Rice at this stage was Terry Horgan, a public relations practitioner from Castleknock, County Dublin, who would later become a prime mover in the founding of a new lay catholic network, Family Solidarity. Mr Horgan is mentioned in a book published in Ireland in 1989 on the catholic lay organisation, Opus Dei, called *The Work*, as one of three key figures involved in the establishment of the Opus Dei Educational Development Trust in the early 1970s. The aim of the trust was to establish secondary schools for girls and boys throughout the country. He was described in the book as a director of Murray Consultants, one of Ireland's largest PR firms.

Professor Rice has told the author that Mr Horgan met with him several times in the United States to discuss the abortion issue from a legal perspective, particularly the relationship between family and civil law, and also the complexities of constitutional law in this area. Professor Rice would keep in contact with Terry Horgan, John O'Reilly and lawyers attached to PLAC throughout the entire campaign, advising on amendment wordings.

For a time, Vaughan and her group resisted O'Reilly's attempts to heighten the movement's profile. They believed that too much agitation at this point might prompt the politicians to sideline the issue through an all party committee or some such stalling device. But a very visible weakening of Garret FitzGerald's stance on the anti-abortion amendment forced a re-evaluation of their approach.

In June, a general election had returned another Fine Gael/Labour coalition. The commitment to the amendment had appeared in the Fine Gael manifesto but was absent from the joint programme for Government published in July. The commitment in the manifesto read: 'Fine Gael is unalterably opposed to the legalisation of abortion and in Government will initiate a referendum to guarantee the right to life of the unborn child.'

PLAC immediately wrote to FitzGerald, receiving a reply almost one month later. The new Taoiseach wrote: 'There is no significance whatsoever in the fact that the commitment is not referred to in the document *Programme for Government 1981-86*. The Government is unalterably opposed to the legalisation of abortion and is committed to taking whatever steps are necessary to ensure that an appropriate constitutional amendment is brought forward. The Attorney General is now examining the form such an amendment might take.'

The Vaughan faction accepted the letter at face value while the more militant activists wanted to pin FitzGerald to a date and also to take private soundings from the Attorney General's office to discover the actual state of play.

In September alarm bells began ringing even louder. It was during that month that FitzGerald launched what he dubbed a 'Constitutional Crusade'. In an RTE interview on the *This Week* programme with presenter Gerald Barry, he said that one of his overriding concerns was the sectarian nature of the Irish state. It had evolved not as a place where Catholic, Protestant and Dissenter could feel equally cherished, but one in which the dominant ethos, reflected in the state's laws, was Roman Catholic.

FitzGerald told Barry: 'I want to lead a crusade, a republican crusade, to make this a genuine republic ... I believe that we would (then) have a basis on which many Protestants in the North would be willing to consider a relationship with us. If I were a Northern Protestant today, I cannot see how I could be attracted to getting involved with a state that is itself sectarian - not in the acutely sectarian way that Northern Ireland was ... (but) the fact is our laws and our Constitution, our practices, our attitudes reflect those of a majority ethos and are not acceptable to Protestants in Northern Ireland.'

FitzGerald added that he was not going to rush into a referendum but rather try first to lead the country towards the objective of a pluralist society. If he felt there was sufficient support, he said, he would then hold a referendum not just on Articles 2 and 3 which make the territorial claim on the North, but on the Constitution itself. There would be in effect a cleaned-up, sectarian-free, catholic church ethos-free, Constitution.

It is not clear whether FitzGerald realised the implications of these words on his amendment commitment. The problem to a degree was the lack of any sophisticated intellectual awareness of the complexity of the abortion issue in the country at the time. Apart from a small band of committed feminists, few people had ever thought it through. Abortion was simply wrong in all cases, save when a woman's life was threatened (and even that wasn't clearcut as the Hodgers case would show) and every politician, including the academically brilliant FitzGerald, believed themselves to be on non-sectarian *terra firma* when they stated their unqualified opposition to the direct termination of a pregnancy.

Within PLAC, there were heated discussions on the implications of FitzGerald's fledgling crusade. Some were concerned that his intention to table a number of amendments to the Constitution would delay the enactment of the anti-abortion referendum. Professor O'Leary in particular wanted to hang tough. PLAC minutes (as recorded in Hesketh's book)

73

state: 'In reply Professor O'Leary said there might well be a majority in the Government in favour of the amendment. He felt (however) that the (PLAC) executive had been too anxious to apply the kid-glove treatment in dealing with the Government. The fact of the matter was that politicians were a thick-skinned group. He said that we are a recognised lobby and that we should use the tactics of the lobby in forcing the Government to act. This was the very stuff of politics. He very strongly urged that we should be vocal in our condemnation of the Government if the legislation was not brought forward. We should publicise the (Fitgerald) letter and we should also, privately, get in touch with the office of the Attorney General to find out precisely what state the proposed amendment had reached.'

Nonetheless, the hardliners failed to win the day. The gentle approach continued for a number of weeks in the hope that FitzGerald, without further prompting, would simply comply with his commitment.

But a meeting between PLAC and FitzGerald on 10 December disabused them of that. At that meeting attended by Julia Vaughan, PLAC patrons Professor Kieran O'Driscoll and Professor Eamon O'Dwyer, Denis Barror and John Blayney SC, FitzGerald stated that the amendment would form part of an overall review of the Constitution which might take place in two years time, in 1983.

Pressed to take a separate stance on the anti-abortion amendment FitzGerald agreed to reconsider, promising in the meantime to initiate prohibitive abortion legislation in the event of the 1862 Offences Against the Person Act (which prohibits abortion) being challenged in the courts. He told PLAC he would respond in two months, but seven weeks later, in January 1982, the Coalition Government fell after a Dáil defeat on the budget.

The subsequent general election, and the events of the following months, marked the growing politicisation of the amendment campaign, with Fianna Fáil eager to depict Fine Gael as closet pro-abortionists and Garret FitzGerald singularly failing to reach, or articulate, a clearcut position on the issue. The period is also notable for the largely unquestioning acceptance by the politicians of the right of PLAC to make demands on the issue, and of their consequent duty to act when PLAC demanded they should.

The February 1982 election brought a new round of letters to party leaders from PLAC. These letters demanded that the leaders state whether they would hold a referendum during the next Dáil session (ie before July 1982), irrespective of whether or not the proposed review of the entire Constitution was ready.

FitGerald replied: '... the purpose of this letter is again to confirm, unequivocally, my commitment to protect the right to life of the unborn child. I have already specifically instructed the Attorney General to examine the Constitution with a view to advising me as to the best method of ensuring that the right to life of an unborn child will have constitutional protection. I will take such steps as are necessary to provide constitutional protection for the unborn child during the course of the next Dáil.'

What FitzGerald was very obviously doing was kicking for touch. By now he had realised the potential conflict between his 'Pro-Life' commitment and his constitutional crusade. He did not rule out his plan to include an anti-abortion amendment as part of an overall review, which PLAC did not want, nor did he agree to introduce such an amendment during the next Dáil session, but rather during the next five year Dáil term.

Charles Haughey's response was unequivocally accepting of the PLAC demands. Never one to miss a sure-fire populist cause, Haughey did not pause either to examine his own or the non-Catholic conscience on abortion before embracing the fundamentalism of the PLAC position. He wrote: 'I am glad to be able to confirm to your executive committee that when elected to office the new Fianna Fáil Government will arrange to have the necessary legislation for a proposed constitutional amendment to guarantee the right of life of the foetus initiated in Dáil Eireann during the course of this year, 1982, without reference to any other aspect of constitutional change.'

Haughey, narrowly, won the election. In the months that followed, it was FitzGerald who was continually interrogated on his stance to the proposed amendment. Asked on radio, in May 1982, why he contemplated holding an anti-abortion referendum but only in tandem with other constitutional changes, he replied that the Protestant community in Northern Ireland might react negatively to the amendment if taken in isolation, on the grounds that it could be seen as sectarian.

But ever anxious to reassert his anti-abortion credentials, Dr FitzGerald spoke in June of the inadequacy of the Constitution in relation to guaranteeing the right to life of the foetus. FitzGerald was clearly attempting to have his cake and eat it. If the amendment was potentially sectarian, then its inclusion as part of a review package was hardly going to mitigate its sectarian nature. And, if this was so, then the logic of FitzGerald's position even at this point was to scrap the amendment idea altogether. It was simply nonsense to suggest that everything would be fine if a handful of non-sectarian minor amendments were also placed in the constitutional melting pot.

FitzGerald was simply terrified, with some justification, of being depicted as "soft" on abortion if he did a complete U turn on the abortion issue. With the amendment very firmly in the political arena, he was aware of the dangerous and combustible force of a PLAC alliance with Fianna Fáil. PLAC were now calling the shots, with the power to make or break FitzGerald or any politician who stood in their way. The fanatical, fundamentalist roots of the organisation were neither questioned nor uncovered. John O'Reilly and his Opus Dei/Knights of Columbanus puppet-masters pulled the strings far from the public gaze. The medical and legal puppets presented the acceptable face of the movement which few politicians felt safe in ignoring.

The extent to which Fianna Fáil was prepared, with nauseating relish, to use the abortion issue as a stick with which to lash Fine Gael became quickly apparent. In September 1982 a report appeared in the *Sunday Press* newspaper claiming that the party's spokeswoman on women's affairs, Nuala Fennell, had told an Irish gathering in San Francisco that under a Fine Gael/Labour Government the anti-abortion amendment would be allowed to lapse. Despite Nuala Fennell's trenchant denials of the report, her alleged remarks provoked a huge negative reaction, not least within her own party. TD Tom O'Donnell, a 'Pro-Life' supporter and brother of PLAC activist, Bernadette Bonar, said her views must be challenged.

Fianna Fáil minister Paddy Power queried where Fine Gael stood on abortion, a line taken up with gleeful alacrity by another Fianna Fáil minister Pádraig Flynn who claimed that there was a tacit acceptance by the Fine Gael leadership on the need to introduce abortion in certain limited circumstances. Under pressure, FitzGerald had to repeat in public his 'I'm against abortion in all circumstances' line and he also claimed that he was now the victim of a nationwide whispering campaign. Which of course he was.

The complete lack of trust in FitzGerald by PLAC was reflected later that month in a comment in the *Catholic Standard* magazine which stated: 'Pro-Life circles are speculating this week that the episode (Nuala Fennell's alleged remarks) may have been a "kite-flying" exercise by Fine Gael to test the strength of public opposition to any sign of further weakening in the party's commitment to the amendment.'

FitzGerald's position was also being questioned in liberal circles. His continued, albeit lukewarm, support for an abortion amendment was held to be incompatible with his support for a non-sectarian Constitution. Former Government minister and now political commentator Conor Cruise O'Brien wrote: '... For Garret's crusade commits him to removing specifically Catholic provisions in the Constitution. He can't now start shoving new specifically Catholic provisions in it. In terms of crusading (secular style) he would look like Richard the Lionheart embracing Islam.'

But FitzGerald at that stage could not summon up the level of courage that was demanded. Telling PLAC to forget their demands would have provoked a feeding frenzy within Fianna Fáil. And accusing that party of sectarianism was hardly an emotional match for the counter taunt of being 'soft' on abortion. In 1983, any suggestion that a politician supported abortion was the kiss of political death. It boiled down to a question of honesty and courage - the honesty to admit that when forced to confront the complexity of the abortion issue some people did see a justification for it in cases of rape, incest and other tragic situations.

But that was too much to ask of FitzGerald. And on he staggered, incapable of satisfying either lobby. Prior to the Fine Gael Ard Fheis in October 1982, FitzGerald held a meeting with the Irish Council of Churches, at the request of the party leader. The gathering included prominent members of the non-catholic religions. According to the account in Tom Hesketh's book, during the meeting FitzGerald produced a draft amendment to Article 40.2.3 which guaranteed to 'protect the life of the person, born or unborn'. The delegates were somewhat taken aback given their belief, on the basis of FitzGerald's statements over the last few months, that he was in no hurry to do anything about the amendment.

In his book, Hesketh states that some of those present felt afterwards that they may not have fully conveyed to FitzGerald their opposition to the enactment of *any* amendment, irrespective of its wording. However, Hesketh himself doubts FitzGerald's sincerity on the issue at this stage as his advisor Peter Sutherland, the former Attorney General and a close personal friend, had been advising against an amendment since late 1981.

In his leader's address during the Ard Fheis on October 16, FitzGerald again laid stress on his pluralist constitutional crusade. Yet he also pledged his equal support for a demonstrably sectarian amendment as part of that crusade 'package', stating: 'All life, whether of citizens or of people of other nationalities, whether born or unborn, should be protected by our Constitution, (and we must) now tackle the defective form of the existing provisions ... which purport to protect only the life of the citizen.' A motion calling for the effective scrapping of the proposed amendment was opposed by the leadership on the grounds that while they had difficulties to resolve in relation to the type and timing of an amendment, they had no difficulties with its central thrust.

Barbara Cahalane, whose Dublin South constituency had proposed the motion, summed up the disgust felt by the anti-amendment lobby at FitzGerald's fence-sitting when she stated: 'A wave of hysteria has hit the country about abortion. It is regrettable to see Fine Gael TDs had succumbed to this hysteria rather than looking at the problem logically. They had let themselves be cowed into silence for fear of being called pro-abortionists.'

The embattled leader was also getting abuse from the other lobby, the *Irish Catholic* stating: 'With the possibility of a general election in the not too distant future, it is disturbing to find the Fine Gael Ard Fheis hedging on the Pro-Life amendment to the Constitution ... It is disturbing to find their spokesman on justice making clear that the party favours a delaying of the amendment for at least another year or until a set of constitutional changes were put to the electorate.' FitzGerald's doomed attempts to argue the sectarian nature of an amendment he was simultaneously supporting, were causing both sides, understandably, to tear their hair out.

The net result was joy unconfined in the Fianna Fáil camp. The day after the Ard Fheis, Health Minister Michael Woods declared his party's unequivocal support for the amendment. Michael Woods proved convenient for PLAC both in Government and opposition. PLAC's PR man, Brendan Shortall, who lived in Michael Woods' Dáil constituency, was in regular telephone contact, advising the TD on the PLAC line and suggesting on methods of attack in the Dáil.

Shortall would also help to prepare scripts for Fianna Fáil senators Eoin Ryan (Senior) and Tras Honan when the final amendment wording was debated in the Dáil and Seanad.

Questions were also being asked about what other 'non-sectarian' laws FitzGerald planned to produce in his constitutional review. Did it include divorce, pondered the *Irish Catholic*? To add to FitzGerald's woes, his future coalition partners, the Labour Party, despite serious internal division, also turned their backs firmly on the amendment with senior TDs, Barry Desmond and Ruairi Quinn, becoming sponsors of the Anti-Amendment Campaign in August 1982.

On 2 November, just two days before the Government fell, Fianna Fáil published its proposed amendment wording. It read: 'The State acknowledges the right to life of the unborn and, with due regard to the right to life of the mother, guarantees in its laws to respect, and, as far as practicable, by its laws to defend and vindicate that right.'

Almost certainly, Fianna Fáil deliberately published the amendment at that point to provide the party with vital electoral points. The fall of the Government had been signalled well in advance. A minority Government from the start, the death of Clare TD Bill Loughnane and the serious ill health of TD Jim Gibbons had left them intensely vulnerable to the tabling of a confidence motion.

Pushing the abortion amendment to centre stage would put Fine Gael on the defensive. Any fudging of the party's position now that the wording was out, would be touted by Fianna Fáil as evidence of a 'soft line' on abortion. As Conor Cruise O'Brien had written some months prior to the publication of the amendment: 'The real reason why we are likely to get this bill has nothing to do with the right to life, except the right of politicians to political life. Moral issues, in contemporary conditions, are splendid hunting terrain for the hungry, wild dogs of Fianna Fáil. It is a robust and disciplined party. It knows a moral issue when it sees one, and it knows what you do about a thing like that. What you do is, you find out what is the electorally-rewarding approach and you adopt that approach forthwith.'

But what of the wording itself? A study of the immediate reaction to it by both sides of the amendment divide is fascinating in relation to what would happen nine years later when the case of the fourteen-year-old pregnant rape victim came before the Supreme Court - the first time the court would actually interpret the wording in an actual case of unwanted pregnancy. The story of its drafting is equally fascinating, not least because Charles Haughey eventually plumped for a wording that did go some way to meet the concerns of the non-catholic churches and did not take on board the absolutist line of the anti-abortion lobby. To that degree, he can be commended. However, one must stop short at the proposition that it was actually worded to allow for abortion in the case of threatened suicide.

To this day, no one actually knows who drafted the final wording. When the incoming Fine Gael Justice Minister, Michael Noonan, looked for the file in 1983, he found an all but empty folder. The normal discussion documents between Government departments, the Attorney General's office and the Taoiseach's department simply weren't there. They never had been. Whoever drafted that amendment had not worked through the normal channels.

Journalists reported at the time that neither of the two Attorney Generals in the Haughey adminstration had drafted the final wording. In his book, Tom Hesketh, armed with leaked Government memos from 'private sources' states definitively that this was the case.

Haughey's first Attorney General, Patrick Connolly, did submit some sample drafts in June 1982. These drafts met with some resistance from both the Departments of Justice and Foreign Affairs. The sectarian nature of the amendments, plus the potential for conflict with the European Convention on Human Rights were cited as the main causes for worry.

An assistant secretary to the then Minister for Foreign Affairs, Gerard Collins, drafted the following comments on the minister's behalf in September 1982: 'The Minister is of the view that the proposed amendment has serious implications for Anglo-Irish policy, given the ... attitude of the Protestant Churches in Ireland ... given the Government's commitment to fostering reconciliation between the two major traditions in Ireland, it is necessary to examine carefully any proposal which attracts the unanimous condemnation of Unionist politicians who will see in it the introduction of a sectarian provision into the Constitution and confirmation thereby of their view that the state is a Roman Catholic state which aspires to Irish unity, so as to impose domination on the Protestant people of Northern Ireland.

'Reservations have accordingly been expressed about the proposal by Roman Catholics in Northern Ireland (including SDLP Senator Seamus Mallon). The minister draws attention to these reservations and shares the concern of those who hold them that the intended measure will have damaging effects on the image of the state in Northern Ireland and in Britain and will not contribute to the aims of Anglo-Irish policy ... in the minister's view there is some doubt both in so far as Northern Irish and British opinion is concerned, as also in the context of our efforts to present and defend the proposed amendment before the world media, that the necessity for such a far-reaching remedy will be accepted. On the contrary, the likely development is that a hostile opinion of the amendment proposed will be formed in the North, in Britain and abroad without any serious effort being made to understand its motivation. Finally with regard to the possible implications of the proposed constitutional amendment in relation to this country's obligations under the European Convention on Human Rights, while it appears that there is nothing in the convention as interpreted to date which precludes adoption of the amendment, it should be noted that the present state of law in this area under the convention is somewhat nebulous and that the possibility of future challenges on the issue cannot be excluded. The minister submits that these considerations be carefully weighed before the amendment is proceeded with.'

In August 1982 a new Attorney General, John Murray, was sworn in. Leaked memos between Murray and the Taoiseach Mr Haughey showed Mr Murray solidly in favour of a 'Pro-Life' amendment. Murray wrote: 'The right to life generally is recognised as a fundamental personal right both in international law and our own Constitution and it is one which I feel should be asserted positively rather than circumscribed in a negative way.'

Thankfully, Mr Murray did show some regard for the right to life of the woman though not to the degree that he considered her right to be superior. 'It is important that any amendment catering for the right to life of the unborn should not be so framed as to reduce the guarantee of the right to life of the living or to exalt the guarantee of the right to life of the unborn above the right to life of the living, in particular that of the woman. ... While I am satisfied that the rights of the mother are not diminished by the proposed amendment (several drafts of which had now been submitted by Murray) I think it is difficult if not impossible to find an objective criteria which can be put into the text of an amendment which would expressly demonstrate this to be so.' (In other words, how could an equal right to life be given to the foetus which would not lead to a woman's life being sacrificed through a denial of medical intervention.)

Murray continued: 'Therefore a propaganda campaign which was vociferous and repetitive enough might sow seeds of doubt in people's minds as to whether the position of the mother was in fact adequately catered for. While it is a matter for political judgement as to whether such propaganda can be countered I would like to think it should not be difficult to do so but it is a sensitive issue in so far as that the point would be made in the context of the so called sectarian issue, namely the supposedly narrow or limited circumstances under which the catholic church permits an abortion to take place.' (Murray's use of the word 'supposedly' is interesting. The fact is that the catholic church allows for abortion in just two circumstances: ectopic pregnancy, when the egg is fertilised outside the womb and cannot survive, or uterine cancer.)

Throughout October 1982, the Taoiseach's special adviser, Martin Mansergh, held several meetings with members of the catholic church and the Church of Ireland, although Presbyterian and other Church of Ireland officials frequently complained that only a selected few were canvassed for their views.

The principal Church of Ireland contact was the then archbishop of Dublin, Dr Henry McAdoo. According to Martin Mansergh in an interview with Tom Hesketh, Dr McAdoo insisted that the amendment should be positively Pro-Life;

that the woman's rights should be clearly stated; that the beginnings of life should not be defined (ie that the words 'fertilisation' or 'conception' should not be used); that the *status quo* in relation to legal and medical matters should be safeguarded; and that the formula should be worded in such a manner that it should be capable of 'evolution'. (There is no explanation as to what McAdoo meant by 'evolution'. Could it have meant that the amendment would be amenable to different, more liberal interpretations over time as attitudes changes on abortion?)

The draft amendment finally produced did indeed take on board many of Dr McAdoo's concerns. There was no reference to conception or fertilisation, the right to life was asserted positively, the woman's rights were stated though whether this was done clearly or not remains a moot point and, in the light of the 1992 Supreme Court ruling, the wording was sufficiently ambiguous to allow for an 'evolving' interpretation.

It is probably worth noting at this stage that throughout the whole tortuous process of drafting the amendment, not a single woman was ever apparently consulted. Apart from Julia Vaughan it was the men in PLAC who directed their campaign. The political leaders and deputy leaders of the political parties were all male. The Ministers and opposition spokespersons central to the drafting and passing of the amendment, were all male. The lawyers consulted by PLAC and by the Government were all male. The main medical sponsors of PLAC were all male, apart again from Julia Vaughan. The Supreme Court judges, who would later interpret that amendment were all male. The catholic hierarchy, who would so staunchly support the amendment, were all male.

Throughout the entire episode, the voices of women were deliberately and shamefully excluded from the decision-making process. And that decision was about an event - the conception, carrying and delivery of children - experienced only by women.

Once again, patriarchy was dominant.

Reactions

Initial reaction to the amendment wording, finally published on November 2, 1982 was intriguing. PLAC were perplexed. At first glance few of their demands had been incorporated into the text, most notably that the beginning of life should be defined as conception or fertilisation. At a meeting held by the PLAC executive it was, not surprisingly, John O'Reilly who expressed serious concern, supported by Bernadette Bonar.

Ironically, the clauses in the text which spoke of the balance of rights, ie the clauses that in 1992 the Supreme Court would use to assert a right to abortion in this country in the case of threatened suicide, were not those that O'Reilly was worried about. According to Hesketh, O'Reilly was primarily concerned at what he considered the vagueness of the word 'unborn' and the implications of the phrase 'as far as practicable'. Could 'unborn' be held to mean 'from viability', ie from as late as twenty-eight weeks? Could a judge hold that it was not 'practicable' to protect an 'unborn' from abortion if a woman's 'health' was threatened, in the case of rape or incest? In other words was the wording sufficiently tight to ensure that raped women and children could be legally forced to carry and give birth to the rapists' children, or to give birth to the children of their own fathers, grandfathers or brothers?

PLAC's legal advisers, William Binchy, Dermot Kinlen and John Blayney set about studying the wording. John O'Reilly contacted Professor Charles Rice in Indiana to get his view. All were of the opinion that the amendment conformed to their demands - that it would rule out early abortions (ie the IUD), and that the term 'unborn' would be defined as from the moment of conception. In addition the Irish version of the text was held to be even stronger in its language, referring to 'the right of all living before birth to their lives'. PLAC publicly gave its support to the wording one day later. though other Pro-Life groups continued to express caution, lamenting the fact that the words 'fertilisation' and 'conception' did not appear in the text.

Initial reaction from non-catholic churchmen was positive with Dr Henry McAdoo, whose imprint was reportedly all over the text, describing it as 'just and adequate'. Methodist Minister, Rev Desmond Gilliland described it as more moderate than had been expected. The Chief Rabbi, David

Rosen, described the text as 'sensible and acceptable'. The reason for such an initial warm welcome was the lack of absoluteness in the text. The original PLAC text had horrified many non-catholic churchmen. Some even saw in the Haughey text an actual softening of the traditional state line on abortion. Presbyterian Minister the Rev W T McDowell told the *Irish Press* 'I am glad it does not propose a complete ban on abortion. While we are not in favour of indiscriminate abortion, we do concede that in certain exceptional cases abortion is the best way forward.'

The most intriguing comment came from Canon James Hartin, Professor of Pastoral Theology at Trinity College, Dublin, and a member of the standing committee of the General Synod of the Church of Ireland. He told RTE, prophetically, that the amendment could well become 'another lawyer's paradise'. 'I have little doubt about that, especially the phrase where it says "as far as practicable"... I was trying to think, a couple of days ago, what that "as far as practicable" might mean. Well, presumably it could be used to interpret the fact that one must not have laws which would prohibit surgery to a woman, for example, that would be perfectly legal. I wonder, in fact, whether a married woman with several children already who was beginning to suffer from mental derangement and who was mentally ill couldn't in fact come in under that thing, "as far as practicable"...'

Asked to elaborate on this the canon stated: 'I think this wording could include what I at any rate as a member of the Church of Ireland would be looking for. I am entirely opposed to the easy availability of abortion for social reasons ... but at the same time, I think there are a few cases of urgent medical necessity where the need of the woman has to take priority to whatever happens to the developing foetus and I think this is included in this.'

The Anti-Amendment Campaign (AAC) took no such line, attacking the amendment as vague and ambiguous, fearing, in contrast to some Protestant spokesmen, that such ambiguity could only copperfasten the catholic ethos in our contraception and abortion laws. AAC activist (now President), Senator Mary Robinson predicted accurately that the whole abortion issue would end up in the courts. However, she also felt that the wording was unduly restrictive and would rule out abortions in cases of rape, incest and foetal abnormalities.

It was left to Dr Andrew Rynne, also of the AAC, to hit the nail on the head when he stated in the *Irish Medical Times*: 'The amendment ... could bring this country closer to having legalised abortion than it ever has been before ... And so it might well be that we will be treated to the ludicrous spectacle of Pro-Life Amendment people rushing out to vote against an amendment which they themselves had been clamouring for all along.' Rynne even went so far as to state that the foetus had never been under such threat and that even members of the Women's Right to Choose Group were considering voting Yes to it in the referendum.

Labour Leader Dick Spring also stated: 'Abortion could be more readily available than exists under the present legislation.'

Yet some weeks later, by mid-November, the anti-amendment lobby had found sufficient objections to the text to oppose it completely. Their legal people had now concluded that the amendment, if passed, would outlaw certain forms of birth-control; lead to the closure of certain clinics and abortion referral agencies and lead to injunctions against women travelling abroad for abortions.

The AAC was absolutely correct in relation to the latter two points. It could well have been correct on the first point too had not sufficient medical disagreement existed on whether the IUD and other birth control methods were primarily contraceptives or abortifacients. Certainly it was the intention of the anti-abortion lobby to ban those methods if possible and to close down referral clinics. They had also, as shown earlier, contemplated the taking of injunctions but ruled it out on the grounds of impracticality.

Meanwhile, Fine Gael were swift to latch on to the initial positive reception to the wording from a variety of quarters. Just one day after its publication, and without getting any legal or medical advice, the party proclaimed its support for the wording, with Garret FitzGerald claiming that it was along the lines he himself had contemplated. The party also promised that if elected it would hold a referendum on the wording by March 1983. On 6 November, two days after the Government had collapsed, and in a clear attempt to get on the side of the angels on this one, FitzGerald wrote to PLAC: 'I have pleasure in enclosing a copy of the statement which was issued as a result of a unanimous decision of the Fine Gael

Parliamentary Party following the publication of the draft amendment. As you will see, we are committed to introducing this amendment in Government and having it put to the people in a referendum before 31 March next. This referendum will not be delayed by any other consideration. This is an integral part of our programme and will be undertaken by any Government that I may have the responsibility of leading after the next general election.'

And you can't get more craven than that. Other Fine Gael TDs were equally quick to get in line, completely ignoring the objections voiced by the anti-amendment activists. Wexford TD, Ivan Yates, stated: 'In Government we will put this amendment - guaranteeing the life of the unborn child and an equal right to life for the woman - to the people before 31 March, 1983 ... It is the one issue that is *not* negotiable after the election. Let no smear campaign by anyone deflect us from this clear Fine Gael stance.'

The cynicism of the party was stunning. The indecent haste with which they rushed to embrace the wording was motivated by nothing more than short term electoral expediency. Fears that women would be denied life saving medical intervention were ignored; fears that birth control methods, vital to women, would be banned were ignored; fears that women would be injuncted from getting abortions abroad were ignored. It was nothing less than a shameful display of political opportunism most graphically defined in the Church of Ireland *Gazette* some time later when it stated: 'Put not your faith in Princes - aye, but what a pity that those who talk of constitutional campaigns and raise the hope of better days to come should prove to be as empty as the rest of them when words come to deeds.'

A Fine Gael/Labour Coalition Government came to power on 14 December 1982. The earlier commitment given by FitzGerald to PLAC in support of the Haughey wording was included in the joint programme for Government. It read: 'Legislation will be introduced to have adopted by 31 March, 1983, the Pro-Life Amendment published by the outgoing Government, which has the backing of the two largest parties in the Dáil. The Parliamentary Labour Party reserves the right to a free vote on this issue.'

That was December; between then and 31 March, Fine Gael would undergo a painful, tortuous internal process of extracting itself from that promise so explicitly made in its Government programme. FitzGerald's stupidity in instantly acquiescing to the Haughey wording would now come to haunt him as a volume of legal, medical and most crucially of all, Protestant church opinion emerged to damn the amendment and damn him.

In January 1983 came the first hints of a Government wobble on the wording when Labour Party Health Minister Barry Desmond refused to handle work on the proposed referendum bill which was then laid at Justice Minister Michael Noonan's door. Noonan continued to insist that the legislation would be ready early in the New Year and that the referendum would be held, as promised, by 31 March 1983. But by February speculation was growing that the Government was beginning to have serious doubts about the wording as it stood.

On 7 February, Fine Gael Junior Minister Fergus O'Brien said that while he supported the amendment, the wording was still open to change if there were problems. Just five days earlier, in introducing the bill to the Dáil, Michael Noonan had said that while the Government stood over the principle of the bill, they were not committed to a particular form of wording.

On 12 February Garret FitzGerald himself admitted that Attorney General Peter Sutherland had uncovered some difficulties in the wording and that clarification might be needed. (If FitzGerald had allowed Sutherland to comment on the wording when published in November, he might have acquainted himself with those difficulties then. Now, safely in Government, he had finally undertaken the legal scrutiny he should have sought months earlier.)

Naturally, Fine Gael's backsliding provoked an outcry from predictable quarters, with the party forced once again to restate its commitment to an amendment with an anti-abortion stance. The backsliding was unsurprising. Between November 1982 and February 1983 a powerful lobby of opinion had emerged against the amendment. Doctors, lawyers and academics against the amendment formed their own lobby groups to provide an alternative voice on the amendment to that of their professional counterparts in the PLAC lobby. None argued for the right to abortion *per se*, pointing out instead the legal, medical and constitutional difficulties that would arise if the amendment wording were passed. No one felt brave enough to argue the 'right to choose' case. Public opinion on abortion was still largely fundamentalist - opposed in all but the narrowest of medical circumstances. Whatever chance the AAC had of changing public opinion by arguing that women's lives would be endangered, they had no chance in arguing the case for a woman's right to decide for herself whether or not to continue with a pregnancy.

But of most concern to FitzGerald was the united opposition that had now emerged from the Protestant Churches. Even Dr Henry McAdoo, who had initially described the wording as satisfactory, now joined the ranks of those opposed. The Protestant churches, they insisted, had always been opposed to *any* amendment irrespective of what certain individual church members might have thought about the final wording.

It seems clear that one reason for the *volte face* of at least some Protestant church leaders was that under Haughey they would simply have had to live with an inevitable amendment and therefore had to make the best of a bad lot. With FitzGerald however, given his vulnerability on the sectarian front, the possibility existed of getting rid of the amendment altogether.

The most articulate opposition came from the Methodist church who in a statement in late January declared: 'We oppose the holding of a referendum. We love our land and cherish its democracy and are sick at heart that this referendum seems to be going ahead. It may seem undemocratic to oppose a referendum, but real democracy means an open, balanced society in which there is free play for opinion. Democracy is achieved slowly by a process of growing maturity and tolerance and trust. It can be destroyed at a stroke by a doctrinaire edict ... It would be especially unfortunate when we seek a society of open understanding for all of Ireland, that one part of Ireland should be asked to define itself in this respect as a closed society on conservative Roman Catholic lines.'

There it was - the unambiguous charge of sectarianism, a charge which deeply embarrassed FitzGerald given his posturing one year earlier on his constitutional crusade. That crusade had now been subverted by his own political cowardice and ineptitude. By now Unionist politicians in the North were declaring that a united Ireland would certainly be off the agenda should this amendment be passed.

By February clear divisions in Fine Gael had emerged with Young Fine Gael to the fore in deploring the party's position on the amendment. FitzGerald was accused of bringing the state back to the dark ages, of utterly reneging on his commitment to a pluralist state. Dun Laoghaire TD Monica Barnes led the vanguard within the parliamentary party in opposing the referendum. She in turn was opposed by the party's ultra-conservative wing led by Knight of Columbanus the late Oliver J Flanagan TD, and Tom O'Donnell. On 8 February Monica Barnes declared publicly she would not support the amendment and damn the consequences. By the end of February, the party had agreed to change the wording but still hold the referendum. They continued to lack the courage to abandon the referendum altogether.

On 15 February, Michael Noonan had made public part of Peter Sutherland's critique of the Haughey wording. His principal concern was that life-saving surgery on pregnant women might be ruled out, given that the text stated that the foetus had an equal right to life and that no superior right to her life had been granted to the woman. Both arguments, naturally, were dismissed by the PLAC lobby.

Sutherland wrote: 'The meaning of "with due regard to" is entirely unclear. These words are generally perceived to allow for, at least, termination of the life of the foetus in the cases of ectopic pregnancy or cancer of the uterus. The words "with due regard to" have been understood by many to suggest that the right to life enjoyed by the unborn was to be confined in some way. This interpretation is in my opinion incorrect. (The word 'comh ceart' in the Irish text is literally 'the same right'.) The right to life of both the unborn and the woman is stated in the proposed text to be equal and in these circumstances I cannot see how it could be possible knowingly to terminate the existence of the unborn even if such termination was the secondary effect of an operation for another purpose. The issue of intention does not arise in the proposed amendment and thus it seems to me, that even if the termination of the pregnancy is an incidental consequence of an operation to save the life of the woman it would be prohibited. The correct logical interpretation is that the right to life provided for the unborn is absolute. If a doctor were to be faced with the choice as to saving the life of one, and thereby the life of the other, then I believe that the only lawful conclusion to this dilemma would be that he could do nothing, which infringed on either right ... There may be cases where a doctor will have to consider whether he can treat a prospective mother for an illness which might otherwise shorten her life expectancy if this treatment will threaten the life of the foetus. The proposed amendment will in my view tend to confuse a doctor as to his responsibilities rather than assist him and the consequences may well be to inhibit him in making decisions as to whether treatment should be given in a particular case.'

So, not only was the proposed wording deemed to be sectarian, it was also capable of condemning pregnant women to death. At least in the opinion of the principal law officer of the state.

Now came the battle not just to find an alternative wording, but to steer it through the Dáil. In February Sutherland had submitted a proposal which he believed could deal with the major concerns he had articulated over the Haughey wording. His suggestion read: 'The Oireachtas may, by its laws, prohibit the practice of abortion, and no provision of this Constitution shall be regarded as conferring any right to have an abortion.'

At first glance, this wording would appear to take care of the principal concern of the Pro-Life lobby. Ever since the 1973 Roe v Wade case in the USA which had found that the constitutional right to privacy implied a right to abortion, the major concern was that such a right would also be found in the Irish Constitution. And now here was the Attorney General suggesting a wording which would rule out the possibility of any such right being discovered.

But PLAC rejected it nonetheless. Their argument was that while a right to abortion would not be found in the Constitution under the Sutherland wording, neither would an explicit *ban* on abortion. In other words, if the Oireachtas decided to legislate for abortion, according to PLAC there would still be nothing in the Constitution to prevent them doing so. The Haughey wording, on the other hand, or so it appeared to PLAC, did include just such a constitutional ban.

Fianna Fáil, chiefly through its Justice spokesman, Dr Michael Woods (once again conveniently positioned for PLAC), concurred. He stated that such an amendment would not close off the possibility of future abortion legislation.

On 2 March, just weeks before the promised date for the

abortion referendum, FitzGerald told the Dáil that the Government was intent on finding an alternative wording. Fianna Fáil immediately moved to reject any wording that did not include a watertight constitutional ban on the future enactment of abortion legislation. Six of FitzGerald's own TDs, Alice Glenn, Tom O'Donnell, Liam Cosgrave, Michael J Cosgrave, Oliver J Flanagan and Joe Doyle concurred.

That small, but influential sextet represented the old conservative rump of the party, the hangover from the leadership of the conservative Liam Cosgrave, father of Liam Junior. They held to the letter of catholic church teaching in relation to social matters. In addition, they welcomed an opportunity to undermine the new leader who, apart from sidelining their particular wing, was intent on steering Fine Gael in a direction they disagreed with. It was Cosgrave Junior's father after all who had helped defeat his own Government's Family Planning Bill in the early 1970s.

There then began an effective inter-departmental wrangle between the Attorney General's office and the Department of Justice over the precise nature of the new wording. Hesketh's book includes leaked documents from the Justice Department which clearly demonstrate the extent to which the country's top civil servants - all male - were willing to subordinate the life and health of the pregnant woman to that of the foetus.

The Attorney General for example wanted a wording which would give protection to the 'unborn person' but which would allow for medical treatment 'including intervention (in pregnancy) required to (preserve/protect) the life of an expectant mother or termination of pregnancy where the foetus is known (conclusively) to be incapable of viable life after birth'. (The latter is a reference to encephaly - where a baby is born with no brain and cannot survive life outside the womb.)

The Department of Justice rejected the draft. They stated in a memo: 'We do not think the expression "unborn person" meets the published criticisms of the "unborn"... It could raise a major question about the meaning of "person". We think the word "protect" ... is liable to be interpreted as opening the way to abortion *in the interests of the mother's health* ... We have seen no evidence that permission to abort an encephalic foetus would be generally acceptable.' (Author's own emphasis.)

In fact what the Justice Department was advocating was

nothing less than the catholic church view on abortion - that they can be carried out only in two circumstances: an ectopic pregnancy or a cancerous uterus. Cases where the woman's health would be endangered through heart disease in pregnancy, a cancer in another part of her body, multiple sclerosis etc, were not covered in the Justice Department's proposals, nor would they be. 'Preserving' a life was fine - that implied an immediate life or death situation. 'Protecting' was quite another matter. That implied that while a woman might not die immediately as a result of pregnancy (in the case of non-uterine cancer or heart disease) she might still be legally entitled to have an abortion to 'protect' her life from harm further along the road. And that was simply not acceptable.

What the Justice Department proposed was that the right to life of the foetus should be upheld except in 'circumstances where medical treatment or intervention is necessary to save the woman's life'. Incredibly, even this restrictive wording did not meet with catholic church approval. One senior hierarchy figure, as quoted by Vincent Browne in the *Sunday Tribune*, commented thus on the Justice Department proposal: 'There had been no trouble with the first part of the proposal from the Minister for Justice which promised a statement which would recognise that "the right to life exists before birth". What had proved unacceptable, however, was the second statement which (had) qualified the first one. This would have restricted the right to life (of the unborn) in "circumstances where medical treatment or intervention is necessary to save the woman's life". The view of the hierarchy seems to be that such a statement undercuts the whole principle of the desired amendment.'

So there you had it; an unambiguous statement of the catholic church view that a woman's life was effectively inferior to that of the foetus. They could not countenance an amendment which allowed for life-saving operations on women which would result in the death of the foetus. Abortion was fine if it was the choice of the certain death of both during pregnancy or the death of the foetus. In a situation where a desperately sick woman, like Sheila Hodgers, could manage to stagger on in pregnancy, give birth to a child, and only then die - abortion was out.

The arguments went on around the cabinet table and in party rooms. The amendment wording finally agreed, and announced to the Dáil on 24 March, went with the spirit of the Attorney General's arguments and not with those of the Justice Department. It read: 'Nothing in this Constitution shall be invoked to invalidate any provision of a law on the grounds that it prohibits abortion.' (A later, and final, wording announced in 27 April, included the phrase 'or deprive or force or effect.')

The wording did satisfy one PLAC demand - that the Constitution could not be used to justify the introduction of abortion legislation. However, as Michael Noonan admitted to the Dáil, it did not tie the hands of future legislators who wanted to bring in abortion without a referendum. He stated: 'I am not saying of course that the text is not open to be criticised. It does leave open the possibility, however remote that may be, that one day in the distant future the Oireachtas could without reference to the people pass a measure which would permit abortion to be carried out.'

And with that statement the game was up. The whole point of the PLAC campaign was to prevent abortion *ever* being introduced without a referendum. Here now was Michael Noonan openly admitting that his wording utterly failed to achieve that. A future Government could introduce abortion without so much as a nod in the direction of 'We The People'.

It was a lacuna pounced on with relish by Fianna Fáil leader Charles J Haughey when he told the Dáil: '... It is not Pro-Life. In effect, all that it states is that the 1861 Act shall not be found unconstitutional by the courts. Everybody in the house should understand that if the amendment proposed by the Government is included in the Constitution, it is no bar to the introduction of legalised abortion in this country. There will be nothing to prevent the Oireachtas the day after that constitutional amendment is made, repealing the 1861 Act and leaving the whole situation wide open and having no protection whatever for the life of the unborn, having no law whatever against legalised abortion. Furthermore if that amendment is passed there will be nothing to prevent any Oireachtas at any time introducing into the country full legalised abortion on demand. For this simple reason and for many others we find this wording totally inadequate and unacceptable.'

The fact that any Government since 1861 could in fact have introduced abortion on demand without reference to the people wasn't mentioned by Mr Haughey. The fact that until the PLAC delegation had entered his office two years earlier, this fact hadn't bothered him one whit wasn't mentioned either. Torn between the fumbling FitzGerald and the raw cynicism of Haughey, the women of Ireland were certainly being given a great deal.

PLAC naturally rejected the wording on the grounds outlined by Haughey. They suggested that the Government was less than willing to offer real protection to the unborn - a smear kept up throughout the remainder of the campaign. The Anti-Amendment Campaign rejected it too on the grounds that it represented a pathetic attempt to cling to the vestiges of a stupid, ill considered promise made two years earlier. And as if that wasn't opposition enough, the conservative TDs in both Fine Gael and Labour now announced their opposition to the new wording and their preference for the Fianna Fáil amendment. In addition a number of other TDs in both parties were opposed to any amendment at all.

On 29 March, the catholic church effectively copperfastened PLAC and other opposition to the Government wording. A statement issued by the Irish Episcopal Conference read: 'From the beginning we have recognised the difficulties inherent in the task of drafting an appropriate form of amendment. What is being sought is to enshrine in the Constitution the right to life of the foetus, a right already enshrined under the Constitution by all citizens. This would assure that no decision to introduce abortion could be taken without a direct vote of the people. The new wording proposed by the Minister for Justice does indeed seek to prevent abortion being introduced as a consequence of the judgement by the Courts. It has, however, been acknowledged in Dáil Eireann that this wording would not exclude the possibility that in the future a law could be passed permitting abortion in some form, without a direct vote of the people. Experience in other countries shows that this possibility is not as remote as it might seem. The Constitution is our greatest legal protection in Ireland against violation of the right to life. Surely the most defenceless and voiceless in our midst are entitled to the fullest constitutional protection ...'

When the two wordings were finally voted on 27 April, the Fine Gael proposal was defeated by eighty-seven votes to sixty-five while the original Fianna Fáil wording was carried, with the help of eight Fine Gael TDs and five Labour, by eighty-seven votes to thirteen. Fine Gael, cowardly to the end, had agreed to abstain on the Fianna Fáil wording, a stricture broken by TDs Alan Shatter and Monica Barnes who voted against it.

The amendment campaign proper began in the autumn, with the date of the referendum fixed for 7 September. Both Garret FitzGerald and Labour leader Dick Spring urged the electorate to reject the amendment wording. Fianna Fáil enthusiastically rallied to the Pro-Life Amendment Campaign.

The anti-amendment argument focused principally on legal and medical objections to the wording. With less than a week to go before polling, Dick Spring summed up the essence of the No campaign. He stated: 'We are discussing a form of words which at best will have no effect and at worst will threaten the life it purports to protect. We are in effect being asked to find the Constitution guilty of not affording protection for the unborn and we may be asked to rectify that fault by depriving the mothers of those same unborn of that same protection. If passed,' he said, 'we have then in the Constitution nothing less than a document enshrining an attitude to women which verges on contempt.

But the subtleties of the anti-amendment argument, the attempt to posit an anti-abortion line while still simultaneously decrying an anti-abortion amendment, was no match for the simple, black and white truths trotted out by PLAC.

The AAC arguments were largely appreciated only by the professional groupings with a good grasp of medical and legal practice plus an understanding of the Constitution. To the plain people of Ireland, the message that this amendment would prevent the murder of little babies in their mother's womb, held far more emotional and dramatic appeal.

The final, eve-of-poll PLAC ad read: 'At the end of the day, this amendment is about preventing abortion - the direct and deliberate killing of individual, unique, human beings. If you want to make certain that this can never happen here without the consent of the Irish people, then vote Yes in tomorrow's referendum.'

Not since the Civil War in the 1920s, had anything proved as divisive in this country as the abortion campaign. Characterised by unprecedented levels of bitterness, bigotry, intimidation and raw emotionalism, it pitted woman against woman, church against church, doctor against doctor, lawyer against lawyer and politician against politician.

Accusations of baby killing were countered by accusations of sectarianism and deadly misogyny. It left Garret FitzGerald's constitutional crusade in tatters and empowered that small group of fundamentalists who had manipulated the political cowardice of the party leaders to achieve a very dubious end. It would give to John O'Reilly, that one man out of whose brain had come the entire pro-amendment campaign, a weapon with which he would wield a level of power even he had never anticipated.

The country voted on 7 September, 1983. Of the million and a quarter people who voted, 841,233 or 66.9 per cent voted Yes and 416,136 or 33.1 per cent voted No.

The Eighth Amendment to the Constitution was passed by a two to one majority.

Aftermath

The Irish Pro-Life movement had achieved a spectacular victory in the eyes of the world-wide Pro-Life movement, becoming the first such group to have inserted in a state Constitution an effective ban on abortion. (Chile was the only other country in the world with a constitutional prohibition on abortion - inserted by the dictator Pinochet in 1976.)

The fact that the Irish people and the Irish politicians had proved easy pickings was glossed over as various PLAC activists gave lectures abroad detailing their successes. For John O'Reilly, the successful abortion campaign was simply the beginning. Within one week of the referendum he was laying the groundwork for the next phase of his work. Step one was to maintain the nucleus of PLAC for future campaigns. To that end he moved to continue the work of the PLAC finance sub-committee. Against the wishes of PLAC activists like Julia Vaughan, that committee did not disband.

From that point, the principal movers within that committee would number three: John O'Reilly, Michael Lucey (general manager of Property Investment with the Irish Life Assurance Company) and Senator Des Hanafin. Hanafin had become PLAC chairman midway through the campaign, a move engineered by O'Reilly to assert dominance over the Vaughan faction.

Hanafin raised approximately £165,000 for PLAC, mostly through lobbying individual donors who had responded to newspaper appeals. As a former fund raiser for Fianna Fáil under Jack Lynch, Hanafin was in an unparalleled position to know the sources to tap. He had contacted PLAC himself in 1983 when their campaign was being stepped up.

O'Reilly and Hanafin would form a powerful alliance. O'Reilly pulled the organisational strings, masterminded the campaigns that flowed from the abortion success, while Hanafin used his political contacts as a conduit for the machinations of his colleague. The two men liked each other. Hanafin was in awe of O'Reilly's insider knowledge of everything that moved in Irish society and could appreciate O'Reilly's reportedly good sense of humour. The gregarious, pragmatic, and influential Hanafin held similar appeal for O'Reilly.

The O'Reilly post-amendment grand plan was first revealed

within weeks of the abortion referendum, at a Pro-Life gathering in Rome in September 1983. As quoted in Hesketh's book, O'Reilly stated: 'The internal stresses in PLAC made it undesirable to continue. Another organisation will however have to be formed; perhaps using the structures and grass roots organisations already built up, if at all possible. We still have many problems. Abortion referral is rife and open. Despite the amendment, the anti-amendment lobby is united and vigorous and will not go away but will continue to press on other sensitive areas. There is room for more caring organisations for unmarried mothers. There are pressures for sex education and for divorce which should be resisted. There are plans afoot to liberalise contraception even further. And, as the amendment vote shows, the attitudes of the media are totally out of tune with popular opinion; but if the media remain as they are, popular opinion will eventually take its lead from the media. There are many things which must be done. We know that if we retire from the fight, the advantage we have gained will be eroded and that whilst we choose the battleground we have the initiative.'

The O'Reilly-led SPUC was also indicating just how far they felt that Article 40.3.3 could take them. Writing in *The Irish Times*, journalist Deaglán de Bréadún claimed: 'SPUC will also seek to have British magazines such as *Cosmopolitan* banned in this country because they carry advertisements for abortion services. They have written to the Censorship Board in the past about such publications and plan to do so again in the near future.'

Indications that the Pro-Life lobby were not about to fade away were also made clear at a Youth Life International conference held at Carysfort College, Dublin, exactly one year after the amendment, in September 1984.

SPUC president Dr Mary Lucey told the gathering: '... I would like to see evidence that our legislators and our Government are intent to implement the Eighth Amendment - to implement it to the full. We gave the right to life to the unborn - we pledged that in our laws and by our laws we would defend and vindicate that right. Have we done so? I suggest to you that our Dáil, that is, our Parliament, has ignored that part of the amendment. If over 5,000 Irish babies are aborted in Britain every year, are we defending their right to life? In order to defend the right to life of the unborn, we must close these abortion referral agencies which are operating in Dublin quite openly and underneath the eyes of the law. These clinics must be closed and if the 1861 Act cannot close them, we must have a new Act that will. Is our Government sincere about the amendment or do they believe in the right to choose to abort Irish babies in Liverpool, Birmingham or London?'

There then was the campaign menu: to lobby against divorce; against the liberalising of the restrictive 1979 family planning legislation; against the abortion referral agencies, and against sex education in schools.

The new organisation through which that work would be done began to take shape just two months after John O'Reilly had unveiled his plan in Rome in September 1983. In November of that year, a private dinner was held at the Royal Marine Hotel, Dun Laoghaire, by a number of former PLAC activists.

The gathering, attended by about thirty people, included John O'Reilly, Bernadette Bonar, Michael Lucey and Senator Des Hanafin. The occasion was to make a presentation to Hanafin for his fund-raising work during the campaign. Michael Lucey was general manager of Property Investment with the Irish Life Assurance Company and married to Dr Mary Lucey, the head of SPUC in Ireland.

One account of this meeting from a private source claims that it was addressed by Professor Charles Rice - the US law professor and Pro-Life activist. Apparently the professor told the gathering that they could not rest on their laurels, that there was more work to be done and that the so called contraceptive mentality had taken hold in Ireland. They should not disband, he told them, but rather regroup. He added that they had lost the contraceptive battle, won the abortion battle and should now set about tackling divorce. However, other people at the hotel gathering do not recall Professor Rice. It seems that the hotel gathering, at which similar speeches were no doubt made, was possibly confused with another private meeting around the same time. Certainly Rice had spent some time in Ireland during the amendment campaign. he did not speak to the media but addressed a meeting of the Knights of Columbanus in Ely House in Dublin and a PLAC meeting in Cork.

What is certainly correct is that, after the dinner, a group of people stayed behind to chat on the steps of the hotel. They were John O'Reilly, Bernadette Bonar, Des McDonald, Michael Lucey and Dick Humphries. They agreed that they should regroup, the plan that O'Reilly had himself announced in Rome two months earlier. A further meeting at a private address somewhere in south Dublin was then arranged.

Some weeks later, a document, bearing all the hallmarks of John O'Reilly's organisational style, was leaked to the RTE programme *Women Today*. It appeared to be a blueprint, in memo form, for the formation of some kind of anti-divorce group. The document was six pages long and entitled 'Towards a Pro-Unity (Family) Group (Anti-Divorce).' A three-tier structure was needed, according to the document, to include patrons, executive committee and office staff. The office staff must be 'docile ... they must do as they are told and only what they are told.' (This was underlined). The office 'as the centre of the whole operation' should have a good address, possibly in the Merrion Square or Fitzwilliam Square district; free rental was desirable plus office equipment supplied by the Christian Brothers. The document stressed that a 'new image is needed', so offices other than those used by PLAC during the amendment campaign should be sought.

The document went on to say that the 'machine' should be ready when a 'big answer' is needed. 'For example,' it stated, 'a certain politician said that the Pro-Life Amendment Campaign could kill women. This allegation was replied to, but in a hopelessly weak fashion. It was then hammered home into the mind of every woman in the country. We need to be prepared for that situation. Get the PLAC lists.'

The document stressed that smaller, more fanatical groups should be kept down, groups like the Knock Family Life Centre, the Irish Family League and the Irish Housewives Union. These groups, according to the document, say things such as "Hang in there baby, I'm voting Yes", things that 'cannot be said by the professionals.'

Nonetheless, the document continues 'We have to try and give small groups around the country something constructive to say, in order for their contribution to be serious and effective.' The group would get in touch with anti-divorce groups in England, the USA, Mexico and the Vatican. They would also contact orphanages and school counsellors for case histories. 'For every 'hard' divorce case, reply with a 'hard' child case result of a divorce.

It seems clear that this document emerged from the Royal Marine meeting and that its author was John O'Reilly. O'Reilly found an ally in Father Leonard Coughlan, a Capuchin friar based in Church Street in Dublin. Father Coughlan had also been planning the formation of such a group and had liaised with former PLAC activist Terry Horgan. Horgan had studied the work of the Moral Majority movement in the USA and had several meetings in the USA with Professor Rice. Horgan and Coughlan had already made efforts to set up a number of 'family' groups in Cork, Athlone and Carlow. The movement was called Family Solidarity, although no public launch had taken place.

In early 1984, the Church Street group met with the Royal Marine group. The latter group, led by John O'Reilly, were looking for a banner under which to organise. They did not want to be publicly identified with the old PLAC group and Family Solidarity appeared to suit their purpose.

Several meetings took place in January 1984 between John O'Reilly, Bernadette Bonar, Dick Humphries (an engineer and former PLAC activist) and Michael Lucey on one side and Terry Horgan and Father Coughlan on the other.

The group soon produced its first 'Aims and Objectives' document, distributed to some 3,000 nationwide contacts - in the main those people who had organised the PLAC or SPUC groups in their own areas during the amendment campaign. The group took an accommodation address at 31 Fitzwilliam Street, a few doors up from O'Reilly's Responsible Society headquarters.

The formation of the 'ground troops' began. A private seminar was held, by invitation only, in Church Street. The seminar's aim was to educate the network of organisers on the issue of divorce. The delegates were addressed by former PLAC activist William Binchy and by Professor Robert Noonan of the Catholic Marriage Tribunal. About seventy people attended.

Between January 1984 and August 1984, when Family Solidarity first went public, the ad-hoc committee, led by O'Reilly, moved to organise on a constituency basis. The aim was to set up a group in every catholic parish, attached to a central constituency organisation. An invitation-only first national conference was held on 16 June, where the issues of sex education, divorce and taxation were discussed. Held in Church Street, the meeting attracted 300 delegates.

In August Family Solidarity went public, running into some initial controversy when named patrons on their literature objected to the unauthorised claims of association. The committee included chairperson Michael Lucey, treasurer John O'Reilly, secretary Des McDonald, vice-chairperson Bernadette Bonar and national organiser, Dick Humphries. Solicitor Gerry Collins became public spokesperson. Gerry Collins would later become SPUC's solicitor in cases against the Well Woman Centre, Open Line Counselling and student groups distributing abortion information.

Father Coughlan was presented as the front person for Family Solidarity. He denied that Family Solidarity had emerged from the Pro-Life Campaign although he acknowledged that 'Some of the same people would be sympathetic to our aims and some of the people who were against the amendment would be against Family Solidarity too.' In outlining the aims of the organisation Father Coughlan declared that the group was against all forms of artificial contraception and would vigorously campaign against any liberalising of the 1979 Act.

Here now was a classic O'Reilly creation - yet another front group for essentially the same small group who had engineered opposition to all social change since the early 1970s. The real movers and shakers, principally O'Reilly, Michael Lucey and Des Hanafin, were well hidden from view. From now on they would plan a major assault on the abortion referral agencies and on groups disseminating abortion information and advice.

O'Reilly himself would move to choose young women to feign pregnancy and go on the abortion trail, with the unwitting help of the Well Woman Centre and Open Line Counselling. The tactic of entrapment he had used with his own two daughters in 1973 would be used again, but this time successfully. O'Reilly's plans for the clinics would be interrupted first by the attempt in 1985 by Labour Party Health Minister Barry Desmond, to repeal and liberalise the 1979 Family Planning Act which placed major restrictions on the sale and purchase of contraceptives. This time Garret FitzGerald was determined to get it right - to amend what he describes in his autobiography as '... this anachronistic and disreputable piece of legislation, which sounded like a late flowering of mediaeval ecclesiastical law.'

The proposed legislation continued to place restrictions on the sale and distribution of contraceptives but gone at least was the requirement of a doctor's prescription for the purchase of condoms or spermicides. Gone too was the requirement that contraceptives be sold only to those using them for *bona fide* family planning purposes though they could still not be sold to anyone under the age of eighteen.

The proposed legislation came in for immediate attack from the conservative lobby with Family Solidarity using its growing nationwide 'cell' network to lobby TDs to oppose it. O'Reilly's long standing plan to have banned both the IUD and certain types of birth control pill - including the morning after pill showed signs of being put into effect. A Family Solidarity statement on the bill declared that there was 'more than a slim possibility that this bill, if enacted, may prove to be unconstitutional.' The kind of 'catch all' amendment which O'Reilly and others saw Article 40.3.3 of the Constitution now to be might have within it the power to ban those contraceptives because of their part abortifacient effect.

A fund raising drive was mounted by the organisation. A national newspaper advertisement stated that the new bill, if passed, would make contraceptives freely available to teenagers; undermine the special position of marriage and the family in Irish society; make decent living more difficult for the young, create more difficulties between children and parents and escalate venereal diseases and allied problems. The ad claimed that the Government had no popular mandate to introduce it and urged those opposed to it to '... contact TDs now to vote against this bill on your behalf.'

Family Solidarity also circulated influential, interested parties with literature to bolster their case. Considerable quantities of International Planned Parenthood Federation literature plus literature from the Irish Family Planning Association was circulated. Medical literature which purported to show the life-endangering effects of certain artificial contraception was also distributed. The proselytising had the desired effect - the board supported the surgeons' motion that 'any new family planning bill should reflect the traditional Christian Irish way of life.'

The lobbying of the TDs went on apace under the guiding

hand of O'Reilly and his Family Solidarity worker bees. The committee decided to 'target' fifteen TDs, mark them out for extra lobbying. A special information pack was prepared for these TDs alone. Members of the committee also personally contacted Government ministers.

Some intimidation (and there is no suggestion that this emanated from Family Solidarity) was quite literally criminal. Bernadette Connaughton, married to Fine Gael TD Paul Connaughton, received a letter threatening that one of their children would be kidnapped should her husband vote for the proposed bill. Another letter said that their house would be burned if he supported the Government in the vote. Fine Gael TD Alan Shatter, a member of the Jewish faith, received a letter telling him that the murder of six million Jews during the Second World War was a lie and that he, Mr Shatter, should leave the country. He was told: 'You are an alien. Get out of our country, you yid commie bastard.'

The catholic hierarchy vehemently opposed the liberalising of the bill with the late Cardinal Tomás O Fiaich stating that no change in the law of the state could make the use of contraceptives morally right. He did, however, uphold the right of the Oireachtas legislators to legislate.

Fianna Fáil returned to the tactics of 1982/83 and opposed the bill with Health spokesman Dr Rory O'Hanlon declaring that the proposals would make contraceptives freely available to any teenager. The Fine Gael and Labour conservative rump also re-emerged to oppose the bill with the late Oliver J Flanagan declaring that TDs who supported the bill would '...answer to God for your actions'. But internal opposition was not as strong as it had been with the abortion amendment. When the vote was called three Fine Gael TDs and one Labour TD voted against the bill, while another Labour TD abstained. The legislation was passed, a victory at last for FitzGerald and a set-back of sorts for the conservative lobby.

The main Family Solidarity movers later admitted that the new bill had caught them unawares; they had not yet organised sufficiently well to counteract it. But the big battle, divorce, was looming now. And from the start, from the early days of the post-1983 campaign, John O'Reilly's primary focus and the focus of his colleagues was the defeat of any move to introduce divorce through the removal, by referendum, of the constitutional ban.

105

On April 23 1986, following a series of meetings with the different Churches by Garret FitzGerald, and following a proposal (opposed by Fianna Fáil) by the Joint Committee on Marital Breakdown to delete the constitutional ban on divorce, the Government publicly launched its plans for a referendum on an amendment to delete the ban.

The proposed bill would allow for a dissolution of marriage where the marriage had failed for at least five years, where no reconciliation was possible and where the court was satisfied that the dependent spouse and dependent children would be adequately provided for. A divorce would also be granted only if preceded by a judicial separation of at least two years. An opinion poll carried out some days later showed that 57 per cent were in favour of deleting the constitutional ban with 36 per cent against and 7 per cent with no opinion.

The anti-divorce campaign was launched on 9 May. By 27 June, the day of the referendum, the actions of that group had reversed the findings of that April opinion poll. A massive No vote was returned. It would be John O'Reilly's second major victory in less than three years.

As soon as the Government's proposals were announced, the core activists swung into action. William Binchy examined the proposed text and quickly formulated two dozen objections to the amendment, of which half a dozen would be central. Binchy would become the media front person, the role played by Julia Vaughan in 1983. John O'Reilly was the campaign's chief executive with the casting vote in all major decisions. Senator Des Hanafin once again took on the fund-raising task, assisted by Michael Lucey. Other leading lights in Family Solidarity, notably Bernadette Bonar, were sent to organise and speak at public meetings around the country.

On April 24, just one day after the Government announcement, William Binchy was on *Today Tonight*, hammering home the first nails in the Government's amendment coffin. The strategy was brilliant - speak not of the rights and wrongs of separation but conjure up instead the miserable vision of the deserted first family. Appeal not to morality but to the rawest fears of dependent women - of their husbands running off with younger women, abandoning the loyal first spouse, leaving her to a life of loneliness and poverty. Voting against divorce was not apparently conservative, but rather progressive in its defence of the rights of women and caring in its concern for the jettisoned wife and children.

The very dependency forced on Irish women by the ethos espoused by this lobby was now being manipulated in the most cynical manner possible. As Liz Sherry for the Council for the Status of Women wrote in a letter to *The Irish Times*: 'To suggest that this amendment will impoverish women is untrue. Impoverishment of women exists because our society relegates women to a subordinate role, and, in marriage, to a dependent status in which society continues to ignore the lack of legal and economic equality which all women should have by right.'

According to the campaigners, divorce was not about separation at all - that could be taken care of through legal separation. What divorce was about rather was the right to remarry 'notwithstanding the fact that such remarriages often have the effect of increasing the injustice and hardship suffered by the most vulnerable family members.' (Family Solidarity booklet.)

And these were the points hammered home by Binchy on the night of April 24, the points agreed by both sides later to have eaten away the Government's initial support. Binchy claimed there were serious defects in the proposals, that first families, particularly wives and children, would suffer, that there were serious implications for property and social welfare. The Tánaiste, Dick Spring, also in studio, floundered in his responses.

The anti-divorce campaign (ADC) moved quickly to organise their troops. At meetings in Dublin 500 nationwide conveners were briefed on Binchy's counter arguments and sent back to the hustings with special briefing packs. Four anti-divorce arguments were isolated with instructions to hammer these home on the doorsteps. These were: that this was no-consent divorce, available to one partner against the other's will; the first family would suffer a diminution of succession rights; that compassion was due primarily to the 'loyal' first partner and children; that the amendment was about remarriage - not about solving breakdown.

If asked about the many thousands of irretrievably broken marriages, canvassers were told to dispute the Divorce Action Group (DAG) figure of 70,000 such cases. The real figure, according to ADC, was 30,000, of whom less than half wanted remarriage. The 500 conveners were also instructed on how to obtain and use electoral registers. All left with bundles of posters and campaign literature. The framework of the campaign was directly analogous to an election campaign run by a political party on a nationwide constituency basis, with tight control exercised by a central office - in this case ADC headquarters under the direction of John O'Reilly.

The DAG campaign, by contrast was shambolic - run on a co-operative basis, poorly funded, with the message by and large directed at the converted rather than the volatile middle ground. According to the ADC, their opponents had just one argument - compassion - while they claimed twenty-six. DAG also lacked the dress rehearsal experience gained by the main ADC activists in 1983.

Government fumbling didn't help either. The legislative mattress needed to protect vulnerable dependent spouses and children was not yet in place and there was no guarantee that a divorced spouse would get the protection the Government promised to provide. Its statement of legislative intent, revised two weeks before the referendum, was not enough.

For the ADC, it was above all a marketing led campaign. The intention was to hold their own support and win back those who had said Yes in early opinion polls. One source described it as 'Machiavellian'; it didn't matter what the arguments were as long as they provoked the right - emotive - response: hostility to divorce. There was, said this source, no point in talking about succession rights in working class areas, and impoverished places like Ballymun in Dublin. So there the focus was on the possible loss of vital social welfare entitlements. The state guaranteed deserted wives' allowance would be replaced by the less reliable maintenance payment. If the paying spouse remarried, this maintenance payment might be reduced. A new social welfare class would be created.

In middle class Foxrock the ADC activists focused on pensions - a lot of middle aged male executives in that area would be in line for big pensions on retirement. How would their wives feel if another woman were to share them at the end of the day? Women sympathetic to the pro-divorce cause were asked if they wanted to be divorced by their husbands against their will? The line was that it would now be easier to dismiss a spouse than an employee. One deserted wife in Dublin said she favoured divorce as she was tired of the 'separated' tag. Would she prefer then to be known, said the activist, as 'the divorcee'?

The street posters were devastating in their emotional impact. 'A divorced woman is like a second-hand car - someone else's headache'. 'Does divorce work? Ask Liz Taylor.' Others called on women not to let the roof be taken from over their heads. Dependent women's most primitive fears were the principal weapon employed. And it worked.

The ADC research was extensive. Conveners carried out opinion polls twice daily in their allotted locality, while computer checks (presumably by activists employed in relevant Government departments) were run on the numbers of farmers and self-employed in the different areas before decisions were made on how to pitch specific allegations about the threat posed by divorce to the different groupings. The threat to property rights featured strongly, with farmers of course being told that the spouse would run off with half the farm thereby destroying the entire business possibly built up over generations.

The objective, said the ADC source, was both subtle and simple: to plant ideas in the community that would be discussed at work, in factory canteens, in the pubs, until they became so copperfastened in the psyche of that community that they were impervious to refutation by the DAG.

Other fundamental decisions were taken early in the campaign. The ADC would leave religious teaching and moralising to the church, and would strive to ensure that perceived religious fanatics were not admitted to the public side of the campaign. 'No priests and no loonies,' was the instruction. Efforts were also made to prevent 'fanatics' gaining tickets to RTE televised debates. And, apart from one *Today Tonight* programme from Galway, where a heckler had to be ejected, they succeeded.

The ADC insisted that no official contact was maintained with the church, yet Des Hanafin and his wife Mona Hanafin did have excellent contacts in the upper reaches of the Vatican. Campaign sources have claimed that a message to the Irish electorate from the pope urging a No vote could have been elicited at any point. In the end it was judged more politic to keep the supreme pontiff off the stage.

On June 26, the country voted. A massive No vote was returned by 63.1 per cent of those who voted, compared to a

36.3 per cent Yes vote, almost identical to the 1983 abortion vote. In just two months, John O'Reilly and his activists had managed to take public opinion through a 360 degree swing.

Closing the Clinics

In December 1986, just seven months after the divorce referendum, John O'Reilly scored another stunning success when the President of the High Court ruled as illegal and unconstitutional the abortion counselling carried out by the Well Woman centres and Open Line Counselling.

The effect of the case led to the closure of Open Line, an end to abortion counselling at the Well Woman Centre and, later, a decision by British magazine publishers to delete ads for abortion clinics and advice centres in Britain from magazines, such as *Cosmopolitan*, sold here.

O'Reilly had taken the decision to attempt to ban abortion counselling services from the start of the PLAC movement though claims from the AAC that this was an aim were dismissed or glossed over by the PLAC activists - unwilling at this stage to reveal the Big Brother approach they were actively plotting.

O'Reilly's chosen vehicle for this venture was SPUC, of which he was a council member. In September 1984, SPUC president Dr Mary Lucey told an international right to life conference: 'We gave the right to life to the unborn. We pledged that in our laws, and by our laws, we should defend and vindicate that right. Have we done so? I suggest to you that our Dáil has ignored that part of the Amendment. In order to defend the right to life of the unborn, we must close the abortion referral agencies which are operating in Dublin quite openly and underneath the eyes of the law. These clinics must be closed and if the 1861 Act cannot close them, we must have a new Act that will.'

A letter worded along similar lines was sent around the same time to the Well Woman Centre and Open Line Counselling. Then the plants were sent in. John O'Reilly, according to a very close associate of the man, arranged it all. Apparently several women were picked and told to go 'on the abortion trail' - quite literally all the way to the operating theatre in the British clinics, opting out only at the last moment pleading change of mind.

The plants went first to the Well Woman and to Open Line, told their false stories, were given counselling and arrangements were then made by the centres with abortion clinics in Britain. On their return, the women, under the guidance of O'Reilly, wrote detailed affidavits outlining what they had done. Armed with the affidavits (in fact only one was lodged and never produced in court because Open Line and the Well Woman Centre openly acknowledged, as they always had done, that some of the women they counselled did go to England for abortions), SPUC then proceeded with a legal action seeking to ban the centres from referring women to other countries for abortions.

A legal wrangle ensued for some time as to whether SPUC was entitled to take the case, given that the group had no direct interest in it. In the end, the Attorney General, John Rogers, deemed to represent the interests of the nation as whole, joined the SPUC action in an attempt by the state to provide proper so called *locus standi* ie someone deemed to have an interest in the case.

The first thing that became clear was that no one, least of all the judges, knew what Article 40.3.3 of the Constitution actually meant. No one could say under what circumstances abortions could or did take place in this country, whether they took place at all, how one could make a choice between two equal rights guaranteed constitutionally, and whether women could be legally prevented from leaving the country to seek abortions abroad.

What would never be fully examined in the court was the issue of abortion carried out in this country on medical grounds, ie in cases where the woman would almost certainly die if the foetus were not aborted. The Pro-Life lobby insist that these are not abortions at all, as the death of a foetus is simply an indirect result of the medical intervention. By acknowledging such cases as abortions they would then have to acknowledge a contingent right to abortion information.

The article said that the state would guarantee 'through its laws' to protect and vindicate the right to life of the unborn. So where, asked High Court President, Liam Hamilton, were those laws? On the basis of his client's instructions, Mr Hugh O'Flaherty replied that there were none. What then, wondered the Judge, did they have to guide them in interpreting that Act, apart from the 1861 Offences Against the Person Act, outlawing abortion?

The case for the clinics rested on the assertion that under the Treaty of Rome, a person had an absolute right to go to another country to avail of the services there. It followed therefore that if they had the right to services, they had a consequent right to avail of information on those services. Not so, said James O'Reilly, junior counsel for SPUC. He asserted that Well Woman and Open Line were not commercial enterprises and that the right to avail of services elsewhere therefore did not apply (ie they had no commercial contract with another country). If they wanted to plead rights under EC law they would have to show that they carried on commercial business in another state and this they clearly did not.

But the single most perplexing issue for the judge was the determination of superior and inferior rights to woman and foetus given that Article 40.3.3 gave each the same equal right. Mr Justice Hamilton raised the matter of the legal right to life of the woman. Where does this come into the SPUC case he wondered? Mr Hugh O'Flaherty acknowledged that the woman 'has the right to life as well, but leaving that aside ...'

Mr Justice Hamilton refused to leave the right to life of the woman aside. He did not see, he said, how he could consider one aspect of the amendment without taking the other aspect into consideration. If both the woman and the foetus had rights, and a decision had to be made about which of them had the superior right, who was to make that decision?

Mr O'Flaherty acknowledged that the issue was extremely difficult and that they didn't know. What they were sure of, however, was that abortions could not under any circumstances be carried out in the Republic.

But the judge persisted. Abortions (for ectopic pregnancies and uterine cancer presumably) *were* being carried out in the state despite the amendment. Isn't that the case, he insisted; yes, it wasn't spoken about, but that was because 'everybody's turned a blind eye to it.'

The judge later asked whether a person had a right to travel to another state with the intention of interfering with the constitutional rights of another person. James O'Reilly, for SPUC, said this was a very difficult question and showed the desirability of having an interpretation of Article 40.3.3. The Judge then asked if the Attorney General thought that the right to life of the unborn was absolute or if there were circumstances in which it could be terminated.

Mr Anthony Kennedy, senior counsel for SPUC, said there was no absolute right to life of the unborn because there was the equal right to life of the woman to consider. Even that right to life was not absolute as it could be forfeited for treason or for capital murder.

So in what circumstances then could the life of the unborn be terminated, asked the judge? That, replied Mr Kennedy, is the seemingly insoluble dilemma of the Eighth Amendment.

The judge then suggested that the two equal rights could come into conflict in certain circumstances. Mr Kennedy replied that the court was in the 'horns of a dilemma' in trying to resolve the case. And this was because, added the judge, the legislature had not introduced laws to deal with the matter.

SPUC later contended that there was no evidence that abortions took place in Ireland, as had been suggested by the judge. The judge was simply *assuming* medical knowledge.

He was not, replied the judge, he was assuming medical practice. There was certainly no evidence, he stated, but he didn't live in an ivory tower.

Later, Frank Clarke SC for Open Line, raised the issue of the possibility of preventing women from leaving the state for abortions. His contribution proved remarkably prophetic in view of what would happen over the next few years. If the judge were to strike down a woman's right to information about abortion, he said, the consequences would be as bleak as they were entirely impracticable. A woman could be restrained from travelling to England, if the court were satisfied that she intended to have an abortion there. A woman could be prevented from permanently emigrating, if it could be shown that she contemplated abortion in the course of her emigration. If a foreign magazine, available here, published an article that mentioned the option of abortion, the editor, publisher, directors and journalist could be jailed.

Towards the end the judge's frustration at the lack of clarity in Article 40.3.3 was visible. Frank Clarke suggested that if there were certain circumstances in the state under which abortions could be performed, then a woman was entitled to information and advice on whether she qualified. But what circumstances and what information asked the judge, clearly confused between his stated assumption that abortions did take place and SPUC's counter assertion that they most certainly did not. The advice would have to be not to have an abortion, said the SPUC legal team.

Women were entitled to information, responded their opponents. But information which leads to what? shot back the judge. Finally he said that if the legislature had failed to clarify the matter of Article 40.3.3 the court had to remedy the situation. He was however in 'extreme doubt as to whether I am the arbiter of public morals'.

By the time Mr Justice Hamilton came to deliver his judgement in the case on 19 December 1986, all his doubts had been cleared up. The judgement focused solely on the right to life of the unborn. No reference was made to the dilemma of how to balance two equal rights which had taken up so much time during the trial itself. Neither did the justice encounter any difficulty in arriving at his verdict through the failure of the Oireachtas to legislate for Article 40.3.3 of the Constitution. Fears expressed about the possibility of injuncting pregnant women from travelling abroad for abortions were not dealt with either.

He first noted that the foetus had always had an inherent right to life with or without the constitutional protection afforded by the Eighth Amendment which, he said, 'merely confirms or acknowledges its existence and gives it protection'. In other words the activites of PLAC didn't seem necesssary. He also upheld the right of the Attorney General to move to protect the public interest by either suing to prevent an unlawful act or 'to protect and vindicate a right acknowledged by the Constitution.' It was a point that would become extremely relevant in 1992 in the case of the Attorney General v Miss X.

He noted the defendants' claim that their counselling activities, which they acknowledged included information on abortion services, were lawful given their constitutional right to privacy, to freedom of expression, and to freedom of access to information in the course of counselling and generally.

He also praised the services they provided, describing the centres as: 'Reputable organisations providing many and needed services to women; their employees are skilled and concerned people and well-motivated with regard to the counselling and other services they provide and consider necessary.'

The defendants' claim that their activities could not be

unlawful as the actual termination of pregnancy took place in a jurisdiction where abortion was not a crime was also noted by the justice. The justice could not ban them, claimed the defendants, because by doing so he would be effectively extending the criminal law of Ireland to cover actions which occur in another jurisdiction.

The justice however, did not agree, and this is where he made the most critical ruling - a ruling foreseen and hoped for by John O'Reilly back in the very early eighties when he first dreamed up the Pro-Life Amendment Campaign. The justice: 'Though ordinarily it is no function of the courts to extend the criminal law, it may well be that where there is a breach of, or interference with, a fundamental personal or human right, they may be under a constitutional obligation so to do in order to respect, and, as far as practicable, to defend and vindicate that right.'

He added: 'It seems to me that, where there is a breach of or interference with a fundamental ... right, such as the right to life of the unborn ... it would be scandalous, if the legitimacy or criminality of such breach or interference could "be decided by a flight over St George's Channel". Obedience to the law is required of every citizen and there exists a duty on the part of the citizens to respect that right and not to interfere with it. The court is under a duty to act so as not to permit any body of citizens to deprive another of his constitutional right, to see that such rights are protected and to regard as unlawful any infringement or attempted infringement of such constitutional right as constituting a violation of the fundamental law of the state.'

In other words Mr Justice Hamilton had found that Article 40.3.3 *did* give the court the right to act in an extra-territorial manner - to take action against Irish people linked with activities abroad which were legal there but illegal if carried out in this country.

Finally the judge stated: 'The defendants, and each of them put pregnant women, contemplating abortion, in touch with clinics where pregnancy is terminated so that they can obtain an abortion if they wish ... Their actions in doing so imply assent to, approval of, and encouragement for the procurement of an abortion if the pregnant woman so wishes ... As I have already pointed out in the course of this judgement, the laws of England and Wales offer no protection to the unborn child ... Consequently, many abortions carried out in England and Wales would be offences if committed here ...

'I am satisfied that the activities of both defendants, through their servants and agents amount to counselling and assisting pregnant women to travel abroad and to obtain further advice on abortion and to secure an abortion. Are such activities unlawful having regard to the provisions of Article 40.3.3 of the Constitution of Ireland?'I have no doubt but that they are,' he said.

So there it was. Another massive victory for John O'Reilly and his colleagues within months of the divorce referendum. All abortion counselling and information was now banned in the state. PLAC's tentacles had now spread wider and would spread wider than they had ever dared admit. Women seeking abortions would now have to travel in ignorance to England, attend clinics they had no prior knowledge of, go through the trauma without the initial, vital support back home of the counsellors in the Well Woman Centres and Open Line.

They still went. Irish women continued to seek abortions in England. O'Reilly and his associates had achieved nothing but the imposition of even further trauma on to the minds and bodies of the Irish women determined to terminate their pregnancies no matter what.

Outside the Four Courts, within minutes of the ruling, a smiling John O'Reilly posed for the press.

Open Line Counselling immediately announced its intention to appeal to the Supreme Court, the final court of domestic appeal and constitutional interpretation. The Well Woman Centre later also announced its intention to appeal. The immediate effect of the judgement was the closure of Open Line Counselling and the suspension of non-directive pregnancy counselling by the Well Woman Centre, which continued to offer birth control and related medical services.

Open Line Counselling established, however, an emergency counselling helpline, offering callers access to pregnancy counsellors and to any information they sought - including the names and addresses of reputable abortion clinics abroad. Open Line founder and director Ruth Riddick allowed her personal telephone number to be used as a conduit to the counsellors. Her action was in breach of the High Court ruling.

The Supreme Court Appeal was heard in February 1988 with judgement delivered by the chief judge Mr Thomas Finlay after a four day trial on 16 March 1988. Open Door argued that the right to life of the unborn was not absolute - that due regard had to be given to the right to life of the woman. Consequently, in the absence of an actual case in which the woman's life and that of her foetus were in conflict, the court could not possibly make a decision on the counselling and information issue generally.

Open Line also argued that information cannot directly cause an abortion to take place, therefore such information could not be actionable. And to advise a person of the existence of an operation legalised by an Act in a neighbouring state was protected by the constitutional guarantee of freedom of expression. Open Line counsel further argued, presciently, that if they were restrained in their work by the court this meant that a woman could also be restrained from going abroad for an abortion. In addition any publication or speech which mentioned or might assist that woman could also be restrained.

The Well Woman Centre put forward similar arguments stating that if Irish citizens have a right to travel to another member state to avail of the type of services in question, then it cannot be unlawful for persons in Ireland to advise them about or facilitate them in exercising that right.

SPUC in its submission said that what happened in England was of no concern to the court - all that was at issue was the abortion referral services operating in this state and whether their activities were legal or not. The main thrust of the SPUC case was that the protection offered to the unborn under Article 40.3.3 was infringed by the activities of Open Line and the Well Woman Centre. They agreed that the right to communicate was a constitutional right but if it subverted the constitutional right to life, it ceased to be a freedom. In other words, the right to life superseded every other right in the Constitution. (What was of course clearly evident in the SPUC arguments and in judgements delivered both by the High Court and later by the Supreme Court was that under their logic, every pregnant woman intent on an abortion could and should be legally prevented from obtaining one.)

In his judgement Mr Thomas Finlay moved quickly to

scotch the right to information argument central to the appellants' case. He stated: 'There could not be an implied and unenumerated constitutional right to information about the availability of a service of abortion outside the state which, if availed of, would have the direct consequence of destroying the expressly guaranteed right to life of the unborn ... I am satisfied that no right could constitutionally arise to obtain information, the purpose of the obtaining of which was to defeat the constitutional right to life of the unborn child.' In other words he accepted the SPUC argument - that the right to life superseded all other personal rights. And, based on that, the verdict was inevitable.

The Chief Justice made the following order: 'The court doth declare that the activities of the defendants (Open Line Counselling and the Dublin Well Woman Centre), their servants or agents in assisting pregnant women within the jurisdiction to travel abroad to obtain abortions by referral to a clinic; by the making of their travel arrangements, or by informing them of the identity of and location of and method of communication with a specified clinic or clinics are unlawful, having regard to the provisions of Article 40.3.3 of the Constitution.

'And it is ordered that the defendants and each of them and each of their servants or agents be perpetually restrained from assisting pregnant women within the jurisdiction to travel abroad to obtain abortions by referral to a clinic, by the making for them of travel arrangements, or by informing them of the identity and location of and the method of communication with a specified clinic or clinics or otherwise.'

The Chief Justice further commented: 'The essential issue in this case, having regard to the nature of the guarantees contained in Article 40.3.3 of the Constitution is the issue as to whether the defendants' admitted activities were assisting pregnant women within the jurisdiction to travel outside that jurisdiction in order to have an abortion. To put the matter in another way ... were they thus assisting in the destruction of the life of the unborn? ... (I)t seems to me an inescapable conclusion that if a woman was anxious to obtain an abortion and if she was able by availing of the counselling services of one or other of the defendants to obtain the precise location, address and telephone number and method of communication with a clinic in Great Britain which provided that service, put in plain language, that was knowingly helping her attain her objective ...'

What was interesting about the case in the light of later events was the argument put forward by the defendants on the absence of an actual case to rule on. The same Supreme Court would, in 1992, find that a suicidal woman did have a right to an abortion, yet in 1988 that Court clearly interpreted Article 40.3.3 as imposing a blanket ban on abortion. If it didn't, then the ruling surely would have made exceptions to the information and counselling ban for those women whose lives were threatened by their pregnancy.

The fact was that the court had yet to be confronted with an actual case of unwanted pregnancy in which the true reality of the impact of Article 40.3.3 would be brought home to the five male judges. In 1988 it was a simple thing to deal with abortion in the abstract with the men untroubled then by a case before them of a raped, pregnant and suicidal child.

Within weeks of the Supreme Court ruling, both Open Line and Well Woman had lodged appeals with the European Court of Human Rights in Strasbourg on the grounds that Article 40.3.3 was incompatible with the European Convention on Human Rights. A crucial article under EC law would be invoked to bolster their case. It was Article 59 which confers a right of freedom of movement of citizens of member states who wish to receive services. And under Article 60, in a case decided at the European Court of Justice in 1984, 'services' included medical treatment. Abortion therefore could come under that general term 'services'.

Within a short time of the critical ruling, British magazines carrying abortion clinic ads dropped them from their Irish editions. The wish expressed by SPUC four years earlier, to have such magazines banned because of those ads, had been effectively granted. (By 1991, under the advice of Dublin City Council's law agent, two general information guides for women - *Every Woman's Life Guide* by Miriam Stoppard and *Our Bodies Ourselves* by Angela Phillips and Jill Raukunsen - had been removed from the shelves of Dublin's public libraries as a direct result of that 1988 ruling. The two books carry sections on abortion. According to press reports at the time : 'A member of the public had complained about them.' An anonymous member of course.)

With victory secured in the Supreme Court, John O'Reilly

and his colleagues were clearly succeeding. First had come victory in the abortion campaign of 1983, then the move to introduce divorce had been soundly defeated. Now, in 1988, they had banned abortion counselling in the state, closed down Open Line Counselling and would shortly force British magazines to censor their own publications.

They decided to go further. During the 1980s, Well Woman and Open Line may have been providing the most visible abortion referral and advice services but they were by no means on their own. In Dublin, both UCD and Trinity College Student Unions, through student handbooks, provided some information on abortion clinics in England and where to go to get advice. UCD Student Union's handbook, for example, had included the names and addresses of organisations which gave direct information on how to get an abortion in England. And UCD students would therefore become the next target.

The influential Pro-Life nucleus of John O'Reilly, Michael Lucey and Senator Des Hanafin oversaw the operation. Senator Hanafin continued to raise money privately for the prosecution of the cases. A total of £200,000, according to the Senator himself, was raised to fight the information and counselling cases against the women's centres and the students in the late 1980s.

It was left to SPUC to actually seek an injunction against UCD Students' Union in September 1988. According to one of the key Pro-Life activists, however, 'SPUC really had nothing to do with it. Other people decided to take the case and SPUC was used as the front, because they had standing, they could be seen to have a legitimate interest in it.'

The injunction was to prevent the union from publishing the new academic year's handbook which SPUC expected would contain abortion information. The case was heard before High Court judge Mella Carroll on 7 September 1988. It was the first time that a case relating to the abortion issue had been heard before a female judge. Justice Carroll was then the only woman High Court judge and was later appointed Chairwoman of the Second Commission on the Status of Women.

An affidavit from SPUC president, Dr Mary Lucey quoted the High Court judgement against the Well Woman Clinic and Open Line Counselling and the subsequent judgement in the Supreme Court. It stated: 'Notwithstanding ... UCD Students

Union intends the distribution of a welfare guide containing information which informs persons, including pregnant women, of the identity and location of, and method of communication with, specified abortion clinics in England.'

On the surface, the case, and the points of law raised, were little different to those raised in the Well Woman Centre/Open Line controversy. In that case the courts had decided that the giving of abortion information in the state infringed the constitutional rights of the unborn and were therefore illegal. The students' had also provided, and probably would again provide, such information and were therefore in the same legal position as the women's centres.

But there was one crucial difference in the actual mechanics of the taking of the case. When the action had been taken against the Well Woman Centre and Open Line in the High Court in 1986, SPUC had had to be 'enjoined' as plaintiffs in the proceedings with the Attorney General. Otherwise they would not have been able to take the case as they were not directly involved in the issues under judgement. The Attorney General was deemed to represent the people of the state, including the interests of the unborn. But this time, despite a request from SPUC to join the case again, the Attorney General refused on the stated grounds that proceedings had already begun.

It took the justice just half an hour to reach a verdict. She said: 'What is at issue here is not the Supreme Court ruling, but the right of the plaintiff (SPUC) to an interlocutory injunction restraining the publication of the 1988/1989 Students' guide.'

She added that SPUC was seeking an injunction on the basis of the 1987/1988 guide (which had contained abortion information), but the contents of the 1988/1989 guide had not yet been made known. SPUC had, she said, in the first judicial put-down of any of the Pro-Life organisations, no right to act as self appointed policemen seeking undertakings from private individuals, and it was the Attorney General, not SPUC, who had the right to move in such a case.

In the most damning line of the judgement she stated: 'I am not prepared to have a self-appointed group step in and take over the application of the law.' But she had a word of warning for the students. This issue had been decided not with reference to Article 40.3.3 but rather on a legal nicety. The fact that SPUC had had no right to take the case did not of course mean that the legal principle they were invoking to prevent the dissemination of abortion information was not valid.

Miss Justice Carroll told the students that she was not advocating disregard for the law. They should study the Supreme Court judgement (in the Well Woman/Open Line case) when publishing the guide, and if they disregarded the judgement they should be prepared to take the consequences.

She refused the injunction and awarded costs against SPUC. But less than a year later the case was back in court, this time by way of an appeal to the Supreme Court against the High Court injunction refusal. And this time, it was SPUC who emerged as victors, with the Supreme Court deciding after all that SPUC did have a right to act as the state's moral policemen and overturning Miss Justice Carroll's ruling.

As one barrister put it at the time, SPUC had now been put in the position where it could police the 1983 amendment on abortion. The issue was now, added the barrister, 'uncontrollable from the position of the state'.

The Pro-Life movement, given the go-ahead by the Supreme Court, were now off again. In September 1989 SPUC (again under the guiding hands of O'Reilly, Hanafin and Michael Lucey), successfully sought an interim injunction against four officers of Trinity College Student's Union, preventing them from distributing student handbooks containing abortion information in advance of a full High Court hearing, again taken by SPUC, seeking injunctions against the publishing and dissemination of abortion information by a number of other student union groups. (The interim injunction was granted by Mr Justice Declan Costello, the same High Court judge who would grant an injunction preventing a fourteen-year-old rape victim from leaving the country to seek an abortion abroad.)

The full High Court hearing was heard on October 11, 1989, once again before Miss Justice Carroll. And once again she failed to find for SPUC, deciding instead to refer the case to the European Court of Justice, in Luxembourg, for adjudication.

The students were represented in court by Mary Robinson, then Senior Counsel and now President of Ireland. She argued that the Supreme Court (in the Well Woman/Open Line case) had not ruled that there was no right to information in this state on services lawfully provided for in another EC member state.

She said the Defendants claimed that they had a right under European law to provide information about services lawful in another EC state, in this case, the service of abortion under UK law. The issue at stake therefore concerned matters of European law and she was therefore asking the court to refer two specific questions to the European Court. One was whether a member state could forbid the giving of information about legal services in another state if the same services were illegal in the first state.

The second question was whether the ban on such information was an obstacle to the right to freedom of information under Article 10 of the European Convention on Human Rights.

Within hours of Miss Justice Carroll's agreeing to refer the case to the European Court, SPUC had appealed her decision to the Supreme Court. The court hearing opened on 28 November, 1989. SPUC claimed that the provisions of Article 177 of the Treaty of Rome (which established the EC) cannot be used to defeat the enforcement of Article 40.3.3 guaranteeing the right to life of the unborn - in other words the EC had no right to interfere in the issue in question and Miss Justice Carroll was wrong therefore in referring the matter to the EC court.

The Supreme Court found for SPUC and ordered the students to stop providing abortion information until the EC court had adjudicated. The Chief Justice, Mr Justice Finlay, accepted the SPUC argument that the students were engaging in activities outlawed by the court in the Well Woman/Open Line case.

Mr Justice Brian Walsh said that Miss Justice Carroll's actions in referring the case to the EC court and refusing the injunction was an attempt to suspend the workings of Article 40.3.3 for an indefinite period. And, in a direct attack on her judgement he added: 'It is not open to any judge to do anything which in effect suspends any provisions of the Constitution for any period whatsoever.'

He added that she had not been obliged to refer the case and could have settled the issue in the case without doing so. Mr Justice Walsh also stated that the EC should not be able to force a member state to allow activities which went against the whole thrust of a constitutional guarantee of protection of a fundamental right.

So, in the space of just a year, the Supreme Court had twice ruled on Article 40.3.3 and in both cases had found that its effect went far beyond the simple ban on abortions being carried out in the state. Even the publication of a telephone number was not permitted or a discussion between doctor and patient of the abortion option.

Senior Counsel would now advise RTE on what they could and could not discuss on air; foreign publishers were censoring their publications destined for Ireland; the public libraries, thanks to an 'anonymous' complaint would shortly remove innocuous women's health manuals from their shelves and agonise over whether the British telephone directories should also be removed for fear of legal objections to the abortion clinic phone numbers contained therein.

Just one judge, Mella Carroll, had succeeded, through valid points of law, to spike the SPUC guns, if only temporarily. And she had been overruled by the gentlemen of the Supreme Court who saw nothing in Article 40.3.3 but a complete abortion ban plus a ban on action that would help a woman secure an abortion even in another state.

In June 1991, the European Court of Justice delivered another victory to O'Reilly and his associates when, in an intermediate ruling by the Advocate General in advance of the full court hearing expected some months later, it upheld the Irish ban on abortion information in the case submitted by Miss Justice Carroll. The Advocate General, Mr Walter Van Gerven, found that the ban on abortion information was justified in Community law under a so called public policy clause. The public policy clause, under the Treaty of Rome, means that member states can legislate as they please, without fear of EC legal challenge, in areas of a 'moral and philosophical nature', which affect the 'fundamental interests of society'.

Essentially Mr Van Gerven said that the decision of the Irish public to incorporate a 'Pro-Life' amendment clearly indicated that the protection of the unborn was a fundamental value for the Irish people. This meant that the ban on abortion information naturally flowed from this and the Government was fully entitled to invoke the public policy protection against EC interference.

The fact that the Advocate General also found that abortion was a cross-border service as defined by the EC Treaty made no difference to his final ruling which stated: 'The Treaty provisions with regard to the freedom to provide services do not prevent a member state - where the protection of unborn life is recognised in the Constitution and in its legislation as a fundamental principle - from imposing a general prohibition, applying to everyone regardless of their nationality or place of establishment on the provision of assistance to pregnant women, regardless of their nationality, with a view to the termination of their pregnancy, more specifically through the distribution of information as to the identity and location of and method of communication with clinics in another member state where abortions are carried out, even though the services of medical termination of pregnancy and the information relating thereto are provided in accordance with the law in force in that second member state.'

It was another stunning victory for the anti-abortion activists. Appalled at first at the prospect of having the case considered in Europe, they now had a situation where the extra-territorial effect of Article 40.3.3 was now being upheld by no less a person than the Advocate General of the EC Court of Justice.

And a further victory was just around the corner, when in October 1991, the full EC Court of Justice followed the advice of the Advocate General and upheld the information ban. The court ruled that while medical termination of pregnancy was indeed an EC accepted service: 'It is not contrary to Community law for a member state in which medical termination of pregnancy is forbidden to prohibit Students' associations from distributing information about the identity and location of clinics in another member state where voluntary termination of pregnancy is lawfully carried out and the means of communicating with those clinics, where the clinics in question have no involvement in the distribution of the said information.'

Real Life Versus The Law

1992 was heralded as a momentous year for the European Community. In December 1991, the heads of state of the twelve member states, had, in the little Dutch town of Maastricht, signed a new EC treaty to replace the former Treaty of Rome - the founding document of the European Community. Now, in 1992, the twelve states would be asked to formally ratify the new treaty which would, in essence, propel the EC towards a more federalist system and diminish the sovereignty of the individual states in many social and economic areas.

Ireland and Denmark were the only two states constitutionally obliged to go to the people directly, through a referendum, to ratify the treaty. The other ten states would ratify through their parliaments.

The Treaty debate in Ireland focused initially on economic matters and the neutrality issue. During the Maastricht Summit in December, the Taoiseach Charles Haughey had focused his energies on securing binding agreements to so called cohesion funds, ie money to bridge the gap between the richer and poorer EC states. A lesser concern was the possible sacrifice of traditional Irish neutrality further down the federalist road. Social issues that were touched on concentrated on the areas of employment and the rights of workers.

But in February 1992, an event occurred in Ireland that would threaten the ratification of the Maastricht Treaty - an event that had its origins in the Pro-Life Amendment Campaign in 1983. It was an event that became known as The State v Miss X.

The story first broke in a short, discreet, front page article in *The Irish Times*, written by journalist Niall Kiely. It had emerged from loose talk in the Law Library - the main office of the country's barristers in the Four Courts where news of interesting or unusual cases is swiftly passed around, often landing in the lap of a journalist with good legal contacts.

The story read simply that the Attorney General, Harry Whelehan, a recent appointment to office, had been granted an interim injunction by the High Court restraining a fourteen year-old rape victim from seeking an abortion in Britain, citing Article 40.3.3 as his justification. The full hearing of the injunction request would take place within days, also at the High Court.

It was a stunning piece of news; lawyers and anti-amendment activists who had claimed since 1983 that such a thing was possible were staggered that what they had believed could never be more than an hypothesis had now emerged as a reality. Throughout the country, a strong sense of revulsion accompanied the breaking of the story. Whatever the merits of seeking an injunction against an adult woman who, through consensual sex, had found herself with an unwanted pregnancy, the idea that a raped child would be so treated was incomprehensible.

Unbelievably, the most ardent Pro-Life activists were equally horrified, though for very different reasons. Such a case threatened to disturb the strong anti-abortion consensus in the country. Harry Whelehan was cursed for his action. Could he not have lost the file when it had been passed on by the Director of Public Prosecution (DPP), said one anti-abortion activist to the author, performed some legal trick to have it disappear?

The days before the High Court hearing were marked by intense political and media activity, though with the latter group extremely nervous about commenting on a case that had yet to go before the court. But what comment there was centred not on the case *per se* but rather on the astonishing fact that the Attorney General had actually taken it. For those, however, who had watched the judgements being handed down since 1983 against the Well Woman Centre, Open Line, and the students, the action of the Attorney General seemed perfectly in keeping with the legal logic employed in those earlier cases.

Three days before the High Court hearing, Labour Party leader Dick Spring wrote to the new Taoiseach Albert Reynolds (only days in office) seeking an immediate meeting to discuss the matter. He wanted particularly to ask him if any information had been sought on the state of health of the mother, who is, he pointed out, 'herself a child'. The Taoiseach refused a meeting, wanting first to hear the outcome of the case. Different legal views were given as to whether the Government could now order the Attorney General not to proceed with it. The short answer was that they could not. The Attorney General is the Government's principal legal officer and attends every cabinet meeting but it had also been established by the Supreme Court that he has a function separate to and independent of that, as the protector of the people's constitutional rights. And in this case he was acting as the protector of the rights of the foetus.

Details of the case emerged prior to the hearing, none of which could be printed for fear of being held in contempt of court. The young girl was fourteen, and lived with her family in a Dublin suburb. Sometime after Christmas her mother noticed that the girl had missed her period. After a number of pregnancy tests it emerged that she was some weeks pregnant. The alleged rapist (no matter what the circumstances are, anyone having sexual intercourse with a minor is guilty of statutory rape) was a family friend whose daughter the young girl frequently visited.

The Gardaí were called in to investigate. The parents wanted the girl to be spared the trauma of a rape trial. They wanted to secure forensic evidence to prove paternity, thus minimising the need for a court appearance by the child. They asked the Gardaí if a DNA test would be admissible as evidence in court. (DNA testing, which finds an individual's unique genetic code from tissue sampling is a relatively new forensic method which can identify beyond doubt the paternity of foetus if samples are taken from both alleged father and baby.)

It was made clear to the Gardaí that the DNA testing would take place after an abortion - on the dead foetus. (It finally took place before the abortion on foetal cells in the amniotic fluid.) The Gardaí simply didn't know whether such evidence would be admissible in court. They would have to seek advice. The case went up the ranks and finally landed on the desk of the Director of Public Prosecutions. He, or somebody in his office, saw at once the implications for Article 40.3.3 and referred it to the Attorney General for his ruling.

The Attorney General had no doubts. The state now had evidence that a foetus with guaranteed rights under the Constitution was about to be aborted. He had to act to prevent it at once. On 6 February, he commenced proceedings against the child and her parents in the High Court and was granted an interim injunction 'restraining the defendants, their servants or agents, or anyone having knowledge of the order, from interfering with the right to life of the unborn as contained in Article 40.3.3 of the Constitution of Ireland on such terms as to this honourable court shall seem meet and just.'

The Attorney General's Senior Counsel in the case was James O'Reilly, previously a member of the SPUC legal team in the cases against Well Woman/Open Line and the students.

But by now the young girl, and her parents, were in England with a booking already made for an abortion. They had left their English contact number with another child at home. The child passed on the number when a Garda rang to inform the family about the injunction. He contacted the parents immediately, telling them that an injunction had been granted. Obviously terrified of the consequences of ignoring the injunction, the family cancelled the appointment and came home. It is beyond imagining what the latest twist in events did to the young girl's physical and mental state.

The case was heard in the High Court, *in camera*, on 10 and 11 February with a judgement expected within days. The presiding judge was Mr Justice Declan Costello. By now media speculation about the outcome of the hearing was intense. At the first of what would become regular weekly briefings for the political correspondents of the national newspapers and RTE, the Taoiseach avoided expressing any personal opinion on the case. He said that a particular course of action had been taken by the Attorney General, that it was an action which had not been sanctioned by the Government and that they had had no prior knowledge of the Attorney General's intentions.

Asked about his own attitude to abortion, Mr Reynolds replied that in principle he was against it. Asked whether this meant in all circumstances, he paused for several seconds before replying vaguely that who knew what the medical evidence in a certain case could throw up. He was extremely careful not to lean to either side of the abortion divide, a stance he would maintain over the next several months. He did not say he was in favour of abortion in the case of a raped child but neither did he say that he was not.

The pressure on the Attorney General through the public outcry on the case quickly became evident. Four days before the High Court judgement on the case, he issued an unprecedented statement declaring that 'any public discussion of the facts or issues' of the case would be in contempt of court. This could mean, said some lawyers, that two people chatting about the case could be brought before the court on contempt charges. The Attorney General added in his statement that: 'The publicity and public controversy so far given to the matter must be a source of great distress to the parties and should cease forthwith.'

There was no reference by the Attorney General to the 'great distress' caused to the girl by her very pregnancy and the fact that she was now a prisoner in her own country, forced to continue with that pregnancy until the men of the High Court, and later possibly the Supreme Court, decided otherwise.

The Attorney General's statement was met with defiance in two influential quarters. Labour leader Dick Spring in a public statement declared that the distress to the family the Attorney General was now trying to guard against was nothing compared to the distress caused by having the case taken in the first place. He refused to cease commenting on the general issues in the case.

In an even more direct attack on the Attorney General, the chairman of the Progressive Democrats (PDs), Michael McDowell, a senior counsel himself, simply said that the suggestion that any public comment on the issues of the case was unlawful was 'in my view, wrong.'

He also stated that in 1983, suggestions that the Courts could prevent women from seeking abortions abroad were 'dismissed as contrived and hysterical'. Now, he stated, the Attorney General clearly saw himself legally bound to intervene in such cases.

Curiously, in the light of later policy declarations from the PDs, Michael McDowell did not suggest that there should be no legal bar to any woman seeking an abortion abroad but simply that no bar should be placed to rape victims. At this stage in the debate, every contribution was hedged with much anti-abortion rhetoric. Even the PDs, some of whom would later declare for abortion in limited circumstances in this country, were scared to voice anything but the consensus line.

On 17 February, Mr Justice Costello delivered his judgement. To the horror of both Government and Opposition parties, of both pro- and anti-abortion activists, he upheld the injunction and ordered the girl and her family to remain in Ireland for a period of ten months. The state in effect was forcing the girl to have the rapist's child with the threat of possible imprisonment hanging over her head if she failed to comply.

The preamble to the final decision by Mr Justice Costello gave a further insight into the facts of the case. He stated: 'The first defendant is a young girl, now aged fourteen and a half years. She has a school friend whom she visited regularly. Her friend's parents and her parents were also on friendly terms. Her parents had no idea that in letting their daughter visit her friend's house she was being placed in physical and moral danger. In fact, her statement disclosed that her friend's father is a depraved and evil man. He began sexually molesting the first defendant when she was less than thirteen years old. Over the months in which it occurred this molestation was continuous and took different forms. In June, 1991, abuse of a serious nature took place and this occurred again in the early part of 1991. In December, 1991, her statement records, he had full sexual intercourse with her to which she did not consent. As a result, she became pregnant.'

The judge then referred to the girl's current mental state. He noted that she had confided to her mother that when she learned she was pregnant she wanted to kill herself by throwing herself down the stairs. On the journey back from London, she told her mother that she wanted to throw herself under a train. In a discussion on the case with Gardaí she said: 'I wish it were all over. Sometimes I feel like throwing myself downstairs', and in the presence of another Garda, when her father said that the situation was worse than a death in the family, she replied, 'Not if it was me.'

The judge outlined how her parents had brought her to a clinical psychologist on their return from London. In his report to the court, he stated that the girl was denying her emotions, had lost touch with her feelings, and that she had 'coldly expressed a desire to solve matters by ending her life'. In the psychologist's opinion, she was now capable of such an act.

The judge's decision was made on four legal points. The first concerned the defendants' claim that since the Oireachtas had not legislated for Article 40.3.3 to regulate how the conflicting rights of woman and unborn reconciled, the High Court could make no ruling in the case.

The judge disagreed, stating that many constitutional rights are protected by the Courts even though no laws have been passed to show how this should be done.

The second concerned the woman's right to life. The defendants' argue that because of the possibility of suicide, the girl's right to life would not be protected if she was injuncted from seeking an abortion.

The judge disagreed. The risk to the woman's life was not equal to the 'real and imminent danger to the life of the unborn'. The risk to the woman's life, he stated, came not from a situation in which surgical intervention would be required to save her life, but rather 'comes from herself'. He was satisfied that the girl's family could help her through 'the difficult months ahead'. So, as far as Mr Justice Declan Costello was concerned, he had now upheld his constitutional duty to have 'due regard to the equal right to life of the mother'.

The threat of suicide, no matter how convincingly made, would never provide grounds for abortion, according to the judge's logic. Suicide, he reasoned, could be prevented by the family. The foetus could have no such protection. As the only proof of suicide is death itself, only the child's dead body apparently would have constituted sufficient proof for the satisfaction of the court.

Thirdly, the justice decided that the girl's right to liberty was not infringed by the injunction. He said: 'If a constitutional right is being abused by exercising it to commit a wrong (as would be the case when travelling abroad to procure an abortion) then the court may restrain the wrongful act even though this may involve the curtailment of the exercise of a constitutional right.'

And finally, on the issue of EC law, he referred to the issue of public policy as understood by the Community and was satisfied that Ireland was free to do as it pleased in relation to abortion law, even when it had extra territorial implications, as abortion constituted public policy and was therefore immune to EC challenge.

The outcry in the wake of the judgement was intense. The then president of the Workers' Party, Proinsias De Rossa, called for the resignation of the Attorney General and the deletion of Article 40.3.3 from the Constitution. Fine Gael TD, Nora Owen asked : 'Does the unfortunate rape victim who becomes pregnant have to actually die before her "equal right to life" is demonstrated?'

Labour Party chairperson Niamh Breathnach wondered; 'What rights has a traumatised fourteen-year-old, or any victim of sexual violence, got in our Republic? What future have they got? What can we offer them to relieve their distress and pain, and to help them rebuild their shattered lives'.

Psychiatrist Dr Anthony Clare observed that the ruling effectively confirmed that 'the foetus takes absolute precedence over the life of the mother'. He accused the judge of having simply and unambiguously placed the right to life of the unborn and the right to life of the woman on a legal scales, weighted them, and found in favour of the unborn.

In private, the Government was just as livid. Here was a police state; here were echoes of Ceaucescu's Romania; here was the whole infernal abortion debate reopened in the most harrowing circumstances possible. The case simply had to be appealed to the Supreme Court. But how? The child's parents had had enough. They weren't prepared to undergo further trauma. The Government had to plead. Behind closed doors, negotiations were carried out with the family's legal team. For God's sake, went the message, make them take the case to the higher court. From the roof tops, the Government shouted that they would pay every legal expense. Finally, to intense sighs of relief all round, the family agreed to appeal.

The supreme irony here was that a Government, 'Pro-Life' to the core, pledged to uphold the right to life of everything from a fertilised egg to a viable foetus, was now enthusiastic in its attempt to find some way to get the child to England and allow her to have an abortion. The Government, naturally, did not characterise it in those terms, but that was the logic of their position. If they sincerely wanted that pregnancy to be safeguarded, why not rest with the judgement which really did uphold the constitutional rights of at least the foetus?

The catholic church, not one whit less anxious than the Government for the Supreme Court to get the state off the hook, let it be known that they too wanted the girl's right to travel to be restored. Judicious newspaper leaks let it be known that the hierarchy's legal team had opined that this was the correct course of action.

The Supreme Court was getting the message loud and clear. The gentlemen do not live in a political and social vacuum after all. The appeal was heard on 24, 25 and 26 of February. On the final day of the hearing, in a move as dramatic as it was unexpected, the Supreme Court allowed the appeal, thereby lifting the injunction and allowing the child to travel to England. She had an abortion shortly afterwards.

The full judgement on the case was not made until 5 March. Obviously, if the appeal was going to be allowed, it had to be allowed as quickly as possible, given the girl's advancing pregnancy.

In the interim, there was huge media and political speculation on the basis on which the court had allowed the appeal. Was it European law or domestic law? If European law, the issue of the right to travel would have been central to the case. If on domestic law, what implications would this have now for Article 40.3.3?

When the judgement was read out in court by Chief Justice Thomas Finlay it quickly became clear that the five judges - Justice Thomas Finlay, Justice Hugh O'Flaherty, Justice Niall McCarthy, Justice Seamus Egan and Justice Hederman - ruled on issues of domestic law. Incredibly, the majority verdict of the Court meant that abortions were now legal in the state. In the words of Mr Justice Egan they were legal when there is 'a real and substantial risk to the life of the mother', including suicide. So far from letting the Government off the hook, the Supreme Court had impaled it on several new ones. They now faced the choice of either legislating for abortion in accordance with the judgement - or seeking to roll back the judgement through another potentially horrendous abortion referendum.

Four of the five judges (Justice Hederman accepted the Costello judgement) had ruled that the equal right to life of the woman would not be upheld by denying her the right to travel abroad for an abortion.

As in other cases on the abortion issue, the question of the balance of rights had been teased out in court. Note in the following exchange the doubt in at least one judge's mind - on the basis of the wording of Article 40.3.3 - that a woman's life does have precedence in a case where both lives hang in the balance.

But note the state's claim in reply - that the woman does have a superior right to life, a claim at variance with everything held dear about Article 40.3.3 by the Pro-Life movement and others since 1983 and one which led to Pro-Life activists declaring in private that the state had deliberately 'thrown' the case.

The claims made in this exchange show clearly the daftness of the proposition that a dependent life can be equal to that of the woman. They also expose the Pro-Life pretence that the abortion of a foetus in the case of ectopic pregnancy or uterine cancer is not an abortion but a mere consequence of surgical procedure.

Mr Justice Niall McCarthy had asked Peter Shanley, SC, for the state, if a child must be aborted if the woman is in imminent danger of death? 'If this is so,' he asked, 'where does "as far as practicable" enter the equation? Do you accept that the Eighth Amendment envisages a "lawful abortion" in Ireland?'

Mr Shanley: Yes, I accept that. Pregnancy may be terminated if, but only if, there is an inevitable danger to the right to life of the mother.

Mr Justice Finlay: Your formula is not a formula of absolute equality. It allows for tolerance. It is an equality until the imminence of death. Who should survive?

Mr Shanley: The Mother.

Mr Justice Finlay: Why? Would you agree that 'due regard' in a broad sense would appear to rest on proper regard for the right to life of the woman?

Mr Shanley: I do accept that. Possibly there are reasons for looking at the whole scheme of rights in the Constitution.

Mr Justice McCarthy: But if the lives are absolutely balanced, why come down on one side or the other?

Peter Shanley made no direct reply to the question - a question at the very core of the whole amendment issue.

In his judgement, Mr Justice Egan declared that it is a denial of the woman's right to life 'to require a certainty of death in her case before a termination of the pregnancy would be permissible.' The Attorney General had argued that only a risk of immediate or inevitable maternal death would justify an abortion. This was rejected.

What the Supreme Court ruling now meant was that abortions for medical conditions other than ectopic pregnancy and uterine cancer (the two catholic church exceptions) could now be permitted because death did not have to be imminent to justify termination.

What implications did this have therefore for chronic conditions which can worsen, but not fatally so, during a pregnancy - heart disease for example or multiple sclerosis? Or for certain mental conditions which could, over time, lead to a threat of suicide?

One legal commentator, Trinity College law lecturer, Gerard Hogan went so far as to equate the Supreme Court ruling with the controversial 1938 Bourne ruling in Britain - a ruling long credited by the Pro-Life amendment as having directly led to the current liberal abortion laws in Britain. In *The Irish Times* on the day after the judgement Hogan wrote: 'In (the Bourne case) the trial judge held that a gynaecologist who had performed an abortion in circumstances almost exactly similar to the present one had performed a "lawful abortion" within the meaning of the Offences against the Person Act 1861 (the same Act which forbids abortion in this state).

'Following the interpretation now given by the Supreme Court to the competing interests arising under Article 40.3.3, Irish law now, in effect, has followed Bourne ...

'It is true that the majority of the judges expressly spoke of the necessity for a threat to the life of the mother (as opposed perhaps simply to a distressed - but non-suicidal mental state) but it is often forgotten that so did (the justice) in the Bourne case when he said: "If the doctor is of opinion, on reasonable grounds and with adequate knowledge, that the probable consequence of the continuance of the pregnancy will be to make the woman a physical or mental wreck, the jury are quite entitled to take the view that the doctor, who, in those circumstances, and in that honest belief, operates, is operating for the purpose of preserving the life of the woman."'

In other words, the judge in the Bourne case interpreted life not just in the life or death sense of the term but rather in the sense of quality of life. An abortion was justified in the case of a woman likely to suffer severe mental stress though not necessarily suicidal tendencies.

Hogan concluded: 'Thus yesterday's judgement, if not quite opening the door to lawful abortion in other compelling circumstances such as incest or rape, gives the medical profession great freedom to manoeuvre.'

However, while the decision that the girl in this instance had a right to travel for abortion, or indeed to have one in the state, the ruling on the general right to travel was traumatising.

By a majority of three to two, the judges decided, in effect, that only those women whose lives were threatened by their continued pregnancy could travel. In other words, anyone not in that category could still be injuncted from travelling abroad for a pregnancy termination. The Chief Justice Thomas Finlay along with Justice Hederman and Justice Egan held that the right to travel was subordinate to the right to life.

But, as the anti-amendment lobby reeled from that shock, the Pro-Life lobby were reeling from the shock of finding that their amendment had actually legalised abortion in the state. And, according to Senator Des Hanafin and Professor William Binchy, who spoke within hours of the ruling, legalised it up to full pregnancy term. Ireland now, declared Professor Binchy, had the most liberal abortion law in the world.

So what was the Government to do? The initial reaction to the Supreme Court ruling was confused. Taoiseach Albert Reynolds had at first thought that the Supreme Court had upheld a right to travel. When he learned that this was not the case, he set about getting a range of legal advice on what options were open to the Government in terms of legislating for the Supreme Court ruling, and restoring the right to travel of pregnant women seeking abortions. He did not, he said, want to preside over a police state.

There was confusion too among the opposition parties. Those that had wanted the abortion amendment changed or deleted after the High Court case now had second thoughts when they saw this latest interpretation of what it meant. The controversy had, at least, forced some TDs into a re-examination of conscience on the whole abortion issue, realising just how grey the entire area was. PD Junior Minister Mary Harney declared herself in favour of legislating for abortion in certain circumstances in the state. Within days she was joined in this view by Cabinet Minister Charlie McCreevy. It was an incredible political about turn since 1983. At that time, even the most vociferous opponents of the amendment scarcely dared suggest that they favoured abortion in certain political circumstances. Everyone in fact tried to pretend that the amendment was not about abortion at all, but rather the finer points of legal and medical practice.

Now at last the truth was out. And for the first time in the history of the state a Fianna Fáil minister had dared to say that he supported abortion in certain limited circumstances. It was the logic of the whole debate, Charlie McCreevy declared. Why was everyone so anxious to get the girl off to England for an abortion if not for the reason that they thought she should have one? And if they thought she should have one there, then why not here?

The Pro-Life activists were appalled at the twist in events. They had to move quickly, move before the Government could decide what steps to take in the light of the court judgement, move to fill the political vacuum with their own brand of campaigning and rally anew the people to their cause.

But a new complication had emerged in the abortion equation - a complication known as the Maastricht Protocol. The history of that protocol goes back to some time in 1991 when the final stages of the treaty were being put in place. One man paying very close attention to the draft treaties published at that time was John O'Reilly.

O'Reilly, as has been amply demonstrated, is a very clever man with an impressive grasp of a wide range of medical, legal, political and social issues not just in Ireland but internationally. According to his colleagues, O'Reilly would have studied those treaties exhaustively, looking for ways in which the new treaty, with its federalist thrust might lead to interference with the state's ban (at the time) on abortion.

Whether he found any explicit treaty clauses in which this might happen is unclear but what stood out a mile for O'Reilly was the fact that central EC competence, or powers to override national decisions in all sorts of areas, would be greatly increased under the proposed new treaty. The possibility existed that EC courts could now move to overturn Article 40.3.3 on the grounds that, as EC citizens, Irish women had the same right as their EC sisters to avail of abortion services.

It was this kind of thinking - that the Irish Constitution itself could be used to overturn the legal ban on abortion - that had led O'Reilly down the Pro-Life Amendment Campaign path eight years previously. Now he proposed an encore.

He approached Senator Des Hanafin and told him of his fears. The Government needed to get an explicit guarantee written into the treaty that the EC would not interfere with Article 40.3.3 of the Constitution. Hanafin agreed. In Leinster House he approached the then Foreign Affairs Minister Gerard Collins - Ireland's chief negotiator of the treaty - and casually asked what the Government was going to do to protect the Eighth Amendment.

Several informal meetings took place between the two men on the issue. They are long-standing, close friends and

Hanafin's views on social and moral issues would be largely shared by Collins. Collins approached the Taoiseach Mr Haughey on the issue and also took with him draft proposals for the EC guarantee, given to Hanafin by John O'Reilly himself.

What exactly O'Reilly wanted is unclear. Mr Collins has claimed in a newspaper interview that the Pro-Life lobby were putting pressure on to have their own wording inserted but that these pressures were resisted. Nonetheless, sources close to O'Reilly say that the final protocol wording was by and large what they had demanded. There was also speculation that what O'Reilly wanted was a full treaty article and this would not be unsurprising.

In fact the major battle was over the insertion of the words 'in Ireland' into the protocol as seen below. This was resisted by the Pro-Life lobby, through Hanafin. The exclusion of those words would have extended the extra-territorial powers of Article 40.3.3. The key issue here of course was that such a private debate should ever have been conducted by the Government with the non-elected lobbyists. What right did they have to make demands and seek consultations when the elected representatives of the people, the opposition parties, did not even know what was going on?

At a meeting of EC foreign ministers in December 1991, Gerard Collins persuaded his EC colleagues to take the protocol on board. It read: 'Nothing in the Treaty on the European Union, or in the treaties establishing the European Communities, or in the treaties or acts modifying or supplementing those treaties, shall affect the application in Ireland of Article 40.3.3 of the Constitution of Ireland.'

It was a sizeable coup for O'Reilly, and once again carried out without those who ultimately did his bidding - the Irish Government - being aware of who was really pulling their strings. Gerard Collins has since claimed that the initiative on the protocol came from the Government, a claim disputed by anti-abortion activists.

An examination of the protocol reveals just how clever O'Reilly really was. The stated fear of the Pro-Life lobby was that the *new* treaty might affect Article 40.3.3 yet, under this protocol, the abortion ban would also be free from interference from courts such as the European Court of Human Rights and other EC institutions, including the European Court of Justice.

Once the treaty with the protocol was passed, it would mean that there would be no point in appealing any abortion judgement to Europe as had been done in the students' case and also crucially, in the case involving the abortion counselling issue, which was still awaiting a hearing in the European Court of Human Rights in Strasbourg.

The protocol was inserted by the Government through stealth. Neither the opposition parties nor the public knew of its existence until after the deed was done. The news in fact broke in Ireland through an article in a British newspaper. Nonetheless, there was little fuss. The country *en masse* had given up on the abortion issue - Article 40.3.3 seemed to have unlimited powers and incredible force. The protocol was just a further extension of those powers which would mark little change from current practice.

But then came the case of The State v Miss X and suddenly the Maastricht Protocol hit centre stage. The protocol now posed problems for both sides of the abortion divide. The protocol was a kind of electric fence around Article 40.3.3, which would render that article incapable of challenge under EC law once the treaty was ratified by all twelve member states.

It had been inserted by the Government at a point when everyone assumed that Article 40.3.3 represented a virtual absolute ban on abortion. Now, under the new Supreme Court ruling what the protocol was defending was an article which had legalised abortion in the state.

The weapon the Pro-Life group had used to copperfasten within Europe the Irish ban on abortion had now turned on them. Worse, if the protocol or Article 40.3.3 itself were not changed, legalised abortion in Ireland would become part of European law incapable of change.

But there was also a major problem with the protocol for the other side. Article 40.3.3, again as newly interpreted by the Supreme Court, did not allow a right to travel for an abortion or to abortion information to any woman other than those whose lives were threatened by pregnancy. If either the protocol or the Constitution were not amended, then a Yes vote for the treaty in the referendum meant Yes to a travel ban and Yes to an information ban.

For weeks the Government muddled through the legal morass, resolutely refusing to state what their ultimate objective was, not just on the protocol, but on the substantive abortion issue itself. Did they accept the Supreme Court ruling and would they therefore legislate for it, or did they reject the ruling and would they therefore seek to amend the offending article to get it 'right' this time? No one would say, least of all the Taoiseach Albert Reynolds.

But, predictably, while the Government dithered, the Pro-Life forces regrouped. John O'Reilly quickly moved into action, meeting with Senator Des Hanafin and William Binchy initially and then moving to widen the scope of his proposed new campaign. Through William Binchy, a meeting was arranged between O'Reilly and Brendan Shortall, the former key activist in PLAC, who would now move to organise the Pro-Life media campaign - selecting speakers for RTE, preparing briefing documents for Hanafin and others and answering direct media enquiries.

On 10 March, just five days after the Supreme Court judgement, the new Pro-Life Campaign was launched in Buswell's Hotel in Dublin, just yards from Leinster House. Two days earlier, an ad in *The Sunday Press* had alerted the public to the new campaign offices off Parnell Square, a short distance from O'Reilly's Dublin Corporation office. It was O'Reilly who had found the premises and who, within days, had telephone and fax lines up and running.

The keynote speakers were Hanafin who chaired the press conference, William Binchy, Catherine Bannon, a young Dublin doctor, and Joe McCarroll of Family Solidarity. And hovering in the background, organising the photocopying and distribution of the press releases was Mr John O'Reilly. Neither his name nor his image would appear in any of the newspapers the following day. He liked it that way.

Senator Hanafin outlined the approach and the demands of the new campaign. The Supreme Court had got it wrong, he declared, had interpreted Article 40.3.3 in a way the people had not voted for in 1983. He said: 'After nine years, the clear objective of the amendment, and the clear consensus of the people, have been defeated by a Supreme Court judgement ... Let us make no mistake about it, this is a remarkably permissive finding: it is not an exaggeration to say that the judgement leaves the way open for potentially widespread abortion, because it would be impossible to sustain a prosecution against someone arguing that he had acted in good faith in believing that a suicide threat constituted a substantial risk to the mother.'

Even legislating for abortion in the narrowest of circumstances would be no use, said the Senator, as it could quite easily be found to be unconstitutional in the light of the court judgement. He made his first demand: 'The only way in which this situation can be resolved, and the will of the people made to prevail, is through another referendum. This would be for the purpose of adding a simple prohibition of intentional abortion to the existing positive statement in Article 40.3.3 of the right to life of the unborn.'

Later the Pro-Life Campaign would make explicit that this referendum should take place in advance of the Maastricht Treaty so that this new copperfastened ban on abortion could then be inserted into the protocol and be protected from EC interference.

At the founding press conference Senator Hanafin referred to the protocol only in relation to the right to travel, stating that it should be amended to allow that right. The Pro-Life Campaign still had no qualms about Irish babies being aborted, as long as it was done overseas.

Questioning at the press conference elicited the unsurprising statement from Professor Binchy that suicidal pregnant women should not be allowed to have an abortion. Asked what his view would be if the woman who was denied the abortion subsequently committed suicide, the professor replied that that would be 'very regrettable'.

The young Doctor Bannon suggested that there were ways of dealing with suicidal pregnant women. Further questioning as to what exactly this was elicited the response that this meant locking them up in a psychiatric hospital or the psychiatric ward of a general hospital. Doctor Bannon pointed out that in such a case her view was that she had two patients, not one, to protect.

Some days later, the Pro-Life Campaign submitted their proposed new amendment wording to the Government. It was a single sentence, to be added to the existing article, stating that no direct abortions could ever be carried out in the state.

Once again, the Pro-Life group were toeing the catholic church line - abortions only in the case of ectopic pregnancy or uterine cancer. Under this wording, women like Sheila Hodgers in 1983, would be legally denied abortions or early caesarian sections to allow for medical control of their non-uterine cancers. Such abortions would be termed direct and as such banned under the Constitution.

The pressure was now mounting on the Government from all sides. They had decided to seek EC approval to reopen the protocol to allow for the right to travel but the opposition parties were demanding that the right to information (banned under earlier Supreme Court rulings) should also be inserted in the protocol).

As the Government struggled, over in Strasbourg the hearing by the European Court of Human Rights into the appeal by the Well Woman Centre and Open Line against the ban on information and counselling had just begun.

Dramatically, at the end of the first day's hearing, the state's legal representative announced that in the light of the recent Supreme Court ruling, the state acknowledged that a right to information did exist in certain circumstances.

Shortly afterwards, the Government published its proposed new wording for the Maastricht Protocol. In a clear rebuff to the Pro-Life lobby, opposed to the right to information on abortion, the new wording did allow both for the free right to travel under Article 40.3.3 and also the right to abortion information.

Pro-life pressure now intensified. An abortion referendum was still at the bottom of the Government's preferred options. But within Fianna Fáil, certain elements, led by Senator Des Hanafin and Senator Eamon O Cuív, a grandson of Eamon de Valera, the author of the 1937 Constitution, were beginning to rally to the Pro-Life cause.

Threats by Senator Hanafin to put the demand for an abortion referendum to a vote were averted by clever footwork by Reynolds' party allies at one meeting, but at another meeting to discuss the timing of the Maastricht referendum, Mr Reynolds was left in no doubt but that a majority of the party wanted the Supreme Court ruling overturned by the insertion of a new amendment into the Constitution.

By April, the focus was still on the protocol. The Pro-Life Campaign was demanding that in the absence of an abortion referendum prior to the Maastricht poll, the protocol should be changed to include a guarantee that any future changes to Article 40.3.3 would also be protected from EC interference.

But the Taoiseach still didn't budge.

Foreign Affairs Minister David Andrews was dispatched to look for agreement to reopen the protocol to allow for the right to travel and information. The response was negative. Reopening the treaty even to amend the Irish protocol would be tantamount to opening a Pandora's box, he was told. If the painstakingly crafted, and narrowly agreed to treaty was reopened for one country, others might then demand to have it reopened for them as well. There was mounting hostility to the treaty in both Denmark and Germany. It had to be protected from renegotiation at all costs.

Back home, the Government threw its collective hands in the air resignedly. There was no possibility of reopening the protocol and everyone must accept that reality. The Government now proposed to hold the Maastricht referendum on 18 June, and after that would move, by another referendum, to assert the rights to travel and information. After that, a third referendum on the substantive abortion issue was possible, but in the meantime they would continue to pore over all the legal options.

The announcement was symptomatic of their entire approach to date - delay making any decision on the substantive abortion issue for as long as possible. The Taoiseach did not want to show his hand on the issue. If the Government took the Supreme Court approach and legislated for limited abortion, Fianna Fáil would split in half. If they took the Pro-Life line and rolled back the judgement through referendum the Government would fall and Fianna Fáil's chances of securing an overall majority at the next election would wither away. What they now proposed to do was promise both sides that they would deal with their demands eventually, but certainly not before Maastricht. In the meantime they would pray that the two sides would trust in their *bona fides* to deliver.

An interesting sidebar to the debate occurred around this point with a dramatic intervention by High Court judge and President of the Law Reform Commission - Rory O'Hanlon. In an article in the April edition of the *Irish Law Times* O'Hanlon had put forward his own proposal for a new amendment wording. It read: 'The unborn child, from the moment of conception, shall have the same right to life as a child born alive.'

Not even John O'Reilly could have phrased it better. It was a sentence which not alone made no reference to the right to life of the woman (unless one accepts that women can be offensively dubbed 'children born alive'), but also, if passed, would rule out all pregnancy terminations even if the woman's life was gravely at risk. To add to the general distastefulnesss of the wording, Judge O'Hanlon had used a nineteenth century cannibalism case in Britain as the principal prop to his argument.

The Government was clearly discomfited by his actions but did nothing. Only when, in a follow-up newspaper article on the judge it was revealed that he was a member of Opus Dei, did Albert Reynolds call him to his office and asked him for his resignation as President of the Law Reform Commission.

The announcement that the Maastricht referendum would be held before the issues of abortion, travel and information were cleared up was met with hostility from all quarters - including the Progressive Democrats who were forced to choose between accepting the Fianna Fáil decision to proceed first with Maastricht - or leave Government and force a general election. Faced down for the first time the PDs chose the first option.

Opposition parties and women's groups, including the influential Council for the Status of Women, declared that women could not be asked to vote for a treaty which, as it stood, denied them the basic right to travel and information.

A group drawn from the old anti-amendment campaign, called the Repeal the Eighth Amendment Campaign, demanded both the repeal of Article 40.3.3 and withdrawal of the Protocol to the Maastricht treaty.

The Pro-Life Campaign moved into top gear, piling on the pressure for an abortion referendum before Maastricht. Fianna Fáil TDs were being secretly targeted, urged to get on the Pro-Life side and persuade the Government to deal with abortion before anything else. The élite at the head of the Pro-Life Campaign, O'Reilly, Binchy and Shortall, were filtering through information on their position to certain TDs and others in a bid, as one source put it, 'to get to the target'. What he meant was that TDs would be used to pile the pressure on the Taoiseach by feeding them Pro-Life propaganda which they in turn would use at party meetings, or through direct conversations with cabinet ministers.

Meanwhile, O'Reilly's groundtroops, through Family Solidarity and other networks were in action throughout the rest of the country. TDs, senators, ministers and local councillors were bombarded with petitions, Pro-Life literature, hideous full colour glossy photographs of aborted foetuses. Senator Joe O'Toole was handed a crown of thorns by a caller to Leinster House.

TDs were threatened with the loss of party nominations at the next general election, ministers were pitted against constituency colleagues more than willing to toe the Pro-Life line if it meant the possibility of unseating a rival at the next election.

And then came the intervention of the catholic church. For some time, speculation had been rife about what stance the church would take. Would they dare to tell their flock not to vote for Maastricht and actually put the entire EC Treaty in jeopardy? The short answer was yes they would. Not that they said it explicitly, but to anyone with half an ear to listen the message that came from the hierarchy was no less than a clear instruction not to support Maastricht if it meant copperfastening into EC law the right to have an abortion in this state. The statement came on 14 April, following a special Catholic Bishops' Conference held in Dublin.

It said that the hierarchy viewed with 'alarm' the fact that the right to life of the unborn did not appear to be on the Government's agenda at the present time.

The statement also spoke, and this was the critical passage, of the Bishops' concern that a situation could arise 'where we would lose the capacity to provide effectively in our Constitution and legislation for the protection of the right to life of the unborn child.'

And there it was, the implicit direction that the abortion issue should be dealt with prior to Maastricht to allow a possible new ban on direct abortion to, somehow, be inserted into the treaty before it was voted on.

For the Pro-Life Campaign, the hierarchy's intervention was a major boost to their cause. From now on they would move to tighten the abortion noose even tighter around the Government. If they continued to refuse an early abortion referendum, they would depict the treaty referendum as a simple abortion poll with a Yes vote tantamount to a vote for abortion on demand.

The Government's 'success' in getting the other EC states to agree to a solemn declaration promising to respect any future changes to Article 40.3.3 provided they did not interfere with an EC citizen's right to travel, appeased no one.

The most elementary scrutiny of what a solemn declaration really means would reveal that it is nothing more or less than a statement of intent - a bit like an engagement to marry. If, in future years, the other EC states decided to challenge any further amendment to Article 40.3.3, they would be legally free to do so. It was a point made with no little fervour both by the catholic church and the general Pro-Life movement.

As this book is published the Maastricht Treaty referendum was still set for 18 June 1992, with the Taoiseach coming under further pressure to delay the date until after a referendum on both the substantive abortion issue and on the right to travel and information.

As the Pro-Life Campaign now moves to a climax and the cry goes out that a vote for Maastricht is a vote for the murder of babies, John O'Reilly faces his greatest challenge to date. Through the actions of that one man over two decades, the future of Europe now hangs in the balance. As the Maastricht referendum comes closer, John O'Reilly is busy directing the Pro-Life Campaign from its headquarters off Parnell Square. William Binchy and Bernadette Bonar are touring the country, organising and hosting lectures on the abortion threat and why Maastricht must be voted down if an abortion referendum is not held in advance. At every venue they show the USA anti-abortion video called *The Silent Scream*.

It is a video, comments Susan Faludi in *Backlash: The Undeclared War Against Women*, in which the truly silent cast member is the mother.

The Battle Is Joined Again

How and why did such a small group of men come to wield such power in Ireland? Why were they so successful when other interest groups fighting for the rights of the marginalised, of women, of the unemployed and of the impoverished continued to get scant access to the corridors of power?

On one level the answer is simple: it was a catholic coup. In a country where a large majority are active, practising Catholics any group promoting what was essentially the catholic ethos as applied to reproduction and other social issues was bound to win widespread support. And any group supported not just by the catholic hierarchy and its network of priests and lay people but also by the largest political party in the state, Fianna Fáil, had a major headstart over their opponents.

In addition, the three general elections held between 1981 and 1983, the year of the abortion referendum, gave the Pro-Life Amendment Campaign unparalleled leverage as they played one party off against another. The presence of a conservative rump in both Labour and Fine Gael also ruled out the possibility of a united political front on the 'liberal' side of the debate and enabled PLAC to target politicians in those parties vulnerable to conservative catholic pressure.

But the conservative assault on Irish social legislation was successful also for less clear-cut reasons. The passage of liberal abortion and other social legislation in the United States of America and other countries came at a point when feminism had established a solid base in the political psyche of those countries. Abortion was recognised as a woman's right, not as a humanitarian gesture to women pregnant through rape, incest, or some other appalling circumstance.

The conservative lobby was successful in Ireland precisely because it struck before a feminist perspective on social legislation had taken hold. The country had not yet developed to a point where it could discuss such issues as contraception and divorce, never mind abortion, on the basis of the concept of a human right or more specifically of a woman's right. Contraception was viewed as a way to limit large families, not as a means through which women could control their fertility and therefore their public and private lives. Abortion in

Ireland to this day is seen as acceptable only when the woman's life is at 'substantial' risk or (and this line is taken only by a brave few), when she has become pregnant against her will. The idea that a woman should be allowed choose for herself whether or not to go ahead with a life-changing pregnancy is still an alien concept, yet it is a cornerstone of feminist belief.

The widespread passive acceptance of the patriarchal nature of Irish society also enabled the conservative lobby to hold sway. Nothing threatens that system more than when women are enabled to take control of every aspect of their lives, public and private. And there is nothing more critical to the exercise of that control than the ability to decide how many children to have, if any, and when to have them.

It is hardly coincidential that 1973, the year when John O'Reilly attempted to close down the family planning clinics, was also the year when the employment marriage bar was removed. And the year that Mary McGee was told she could legally import contraceptives. In that crucial year Irish women were enabled not just to return to the workplace after marriage but to determine family spacing and size. Patriarchal control was suddenly under threat and the fight back had begun.

The approach was to counteract the growing view of contraception as a human right by suggesting that artificial methods were both dangerous and sometimes abortifacient. In addition natural methods of family planning were promoted and with such success that the 1979 Family Planning Act commended their use. The same Act also rowed back the gains that had been made by the pro-contraception lobby by strictly limiting the sale and availability of contraceptives.

The attack on abortion through the formation of PLAC took the form of a pre-emptive strike. Pro-life lobbies in other countries have been formed only after liberal abortion laws were already on the statute books. In Ireland, the attack began before abortion had been taken on bord the mainstream political agenda. The issue had been raised within the women's movement in a low-key way, but widespread public debate was not in process.

With the Irish mind so firmly set against abortion, it was an easy thing to promote and have accepted a means by which abortion could never be introduced without reference to the people. Arguments about a woman's right to choose, the concept of a woman's right to liberty and to reproductive freedom held sway only with a very small number of individuals who could not hope to compete with the crude emotionalism of the tactics employed by the anti-abortion lobby.

The conservative lobby was also well served by the imported expertise of their counterparts in the USA. In order to get past the strong liberal forces in that country hostile to any diminution of women's rights, the USA Pro-Life groups had to develop the most psychologically persuasive of tactics.

In her book on the assault against feminism in the USA, *Backlash*, Susan Faludi quotes from what she describes as the 'primary text of the militant anti-abortion movement', a book by Joseph Scheidler called *Closed: 99 ways to Stop Abortion*. Faludi writes: 'When speaking to the press, his manual instructed, "(R)arely use the word 'foetus'. Use 'baby' or 'unborn child'... You don't have to surrender to their vocabulary ... They will start using your terms if you use them." The Wilke's *Abortion: Questions and Answers*, which became the bible of anti-abortion activists, stressed the same objective: "Let's be positive, if possible," the book asserted. "We are *for* protection for the unborn, the handicapped, and the aged. If possible, don't accept the negative label "anti-abortion".'

Faludi continues: 'In their battle for verbal control, anti-abortion activists also co-opted their enemy's vocabulary and images. The Wilke handbook urged followers to borrow the "feminist credo" of "right to her own body" and apply it instead to aborted female foetuses. At anti-abortion demonstrations, "The baby has to have a choice" became a favourite chant. "Little Ones", an Operation Rescue protest song, called for "Equal rights/Equal time/For the unborn children." Women didn't choose to have abortions; they were "Women Exploited by Abortion", the name of the American anti-abortion group that promised to counsel the "victims of abortion".'

Echoes of those tactics can be found in the Irish anti-abortion movement, members of which have spent considerable time studying the movement in the USA. Prominent members of the USA anti-abortion movement have also paid regular visits here and some years ago a branch of Women Exploited by Abortion group was set up in this country, called Women Hurt by Abortion.

The tactics are now being seen again in the current anti-abortion campaign. In late April, days after the Government had formally launched the pro-Maastricht Treaty Campaign, a woman representing a USA anti-abortion group, Campaign Fortress, appeared in Dublin to address a large anti-abortion gathering. The woman had been conceived through the rape of her mother and was obviously handpicked by the Irish Pro-Life Campaign to counteract the tacit national approval of the fourteen-year-old Irish girl's decision to abort her rapist's foetus. On the *Kenny Live Show* on RTE 1 television that night, she told her host how she would have loved to talk to the girl and get her to change her mind. It was a classic John O'Reilly tactic. Counteract hard cases with hard cases which advance the conservative line.

The tactics, and at times, the sheer genius, of the conservative lobby came most sharply into focus during the 1986 divorce referendum. Here was an issue which was not as clear-cut as abortion. As we have seen, a majority of people were actually in favour of divorce at the outset of the campaign. The tactics used were those of the marketing guru. Points of psychological vulnerability were isolated and played upon. The fear of desertion for economically dependent women, the fear of being 'replaced' by a younger rival, the fear of forced sale of a family farm or property, the fear of loss of social welfare or pension rights. It was a campaign that unashamedly used fear as its primary weapon and it succeeded. The message did not have to be truthful for it to work. The message in fact, even if only half believed by those who heard it, could still work.

John O'Reilly's ability to find and recruit people with professional expertise in areas crucial to his campaign work was another key element in the success of the conservative lobby and one frequently remarked upon by his colleagues. He found William Binchy, a respected lawyer and academic with a particular expertise in family law. He found Julia Vaughan, a respected gynaecologist who quickly gave him an *entrée* to other eminent medical professionals. He found Brendan Shortall, a professional public relations practitioner with specific skills in the application of PR techniques to social, political and cultural matters. He also found Senator Des Hanafin, a brilliant political fund raiser who made sure that money would never be a problem in the execution of a successful campaign or court case. He found a raft of solicitors and barristers who could not only provide crucial legal advice but who could also direct cases taken against his liberal opponents.

The rooting out and recruitment of these people was aided by the tight overlapping membership of many catholic lay groups. O'Reilly himself has been at different times a member of the Irish Family League, the Knights of St Columbanus, the Responsible Society, the Council for Social Concern, the Society for the Protection of the Unborn Child (SPUC), and Family Solidarity. He was responsible for the founding of at least three of those groups. Through these affiliations he came into contact with like-minded activists, many of whom also had overlapping membership with those groups.

Nial Darragh, for example, is a member of the Knights and a founder member of the Council of Social Concern and was subsequently active in PLAC and the anti-divorce campaign. Professor John Bonnar was a founding member of PLAC and a patron of the Responsible Society, which itself was launched at the headquarters of the Knights. He is now active once again in the current Pro-Life Campaign. Dr Richard Wade, a prime mover in the early days of PLAC, is also a member of the Knights of St Columbanus. William Binchy has denied publicly that he is a member of Opus Dei, but there is little doubt that Opus Dei members are heavily involved in the wider conservative activism. Professor Con O'Leary, former vice-chairman of PLAC, has also been the subject of media speculation about possible links with Opus Dei and he too is active now in the current Pro-Life Campaign. As seen in earlier chapters, a founder member of Family Solidarity - Terence Horgan - was also reportedly involved in an Opus Dei-run educational trust fund.

But more crucially O'Reilly and the people he surrounds himself with are now past masters at pulling political strings and manipulating the political process to their own ends. They quickly came to know what motivated individual TDs and Government ministers. They knew their backgrounds, the make-up of their constituencies, whether liberal or conservative. They knew on what issues they were vulnerable, who their opponents were on the ground and armed with all of this information they could quite easily move to bend particular individuals to their will. At the end of the day, their success came down to the brilliance of their tactics and the sheer determination and effort of John O'Reilly and his mentors. They truly are zealots, utterly determined and utterly convinced of the rightness of their cause.

They also have a rare insight into one part of the Irish psyche, knowing what buttons to push, what strings to pull. The message they put out is the message that will have impact. It may not always be entirely accurate. Their fundamental aim is control, the control of Irish society and the creation, or rather retention, of a catholic state for a catholic people. They want the laws of the state to reflect one religion and one religion only. Abortion is merely the latest battleground.

Win or lose this battle, their next target is likely to be homosexuality. They will now seek to prevent any Government from implementing the European Court of Human Rights directive to repeal the anti-homosexual laws on the Irish statute books. They may well succeed, at least in the short to medium term. Already the present Government is running scared despite earlier promises to amend the legislation. In December 1990, the then Justice Minister Ray Burke promised to do so within a year. In October 1991 they promised to do so as quickly as possible. In February 1992 Ray Burke said he hoped to publish his proposals later in the year. In April 1992, the new Justice Minister Pádraig Flynn announced that the issue was not on his short-term agenda.

The tactics used will be those of fear - fear of AIDS, fear of other forms of sexually transmitted disease, fear of child corruption. Family Solidarity have already published a lengthy pamphlet outlining the case against the repeal of the laws, a booklet which reeks of barely disguised homophobia.

The divorce battle is also likely to recommence within the next few years. The conservative lobby believe they would again win the day, despite evidence of a significant change of mood since 1986. The tactics would remain the same. Or rather the one tactic - fear.

It is worth thinking about what Ireland would be like in 1992 if everything the conservative lobby had demanded had been granted. For a start, there would be no access to birth control. Doctors could not prescribe and chemists could not supply condoms, IUDs, certain forms of the pill, diaphragms, or spermicides. Women would have to use unreliable, unrealistic 'natural' methods or spend long years on the pill to the detriment of their health. Family numbers would again increase and the abortion trail to England would almost certainly escalate. There would be widespread censorship of magazines, books, films and videos. Women in particular would be denied access to health books promoting contraception, never mind abortion. Women's health clinics would be shut down because of their contraception services. The Rape Crisis Centres would cease to operate through lack of funding and many more women would be forced to either abort or carry the rapist's foetus because of a ban on the morning after pill. Sex education, such as it is now in schools, would be non-existent. Homosexuals would be actively targeted in the workplace, possibly prosecuted for engaging in sex. Social centres for gay men and lesbians would be shut down.

If this seems far-fetched, think again. Earlier chapters in the book clearly demonstrate how the conservative lobby over the last twenty years has sought to achieve every one of those aims.

Politicians and other activists, principally women, have succeeded in facing down the lobby on many fronts. The right-wing conservative lobby have not succeeded in all their aims but they have still managed to exercise control on many major issues, principally abortion, divorce and legislation against homosexuality.

The battle is now joined again. Who dares to face them now? Who dares not to?

References

Binchy, William, 'Marital Privacy and Family Law: A Reply to Mr O'Reilly'. *Studies* (Winter 1977), pp330-333.

Binchy, William, 'Ethical Issues in Reproductive Medicine: A Legal Perspective' in *Ethical Issues in Reproductive Medicine* M Reidy ed. Gill & MacMillan, 1987, pp95-117.

Bowers, Fergal, *The Work*. Poolbeg, Dublin, 1989.

Faludi, Susan, *Backlash: The Undeclared War Against Women*. Chatto & Windus, London, 1992.

FitzGerald, Garret, *All In A Life: An Autobiography*, Gill & MacMillan, Dublin 1991.

Hesketh, Tom, *The Second Partitioning of Ireland: The Abortion Referendum of 1983*. Brandsma Books Ltd, Dublin 1990.

Irish Law Report Monthly, Court Proceedings, The State v Miss X, Dublin 1992.

Ranke-Heinemann, Uta, *Eunuchs for Heaven: The Catholic Church and Sexuality*. André Deutch Ltd, London 1990.

Tribe, Laurence H, *Abortion: The Clash of Absolutes*. W W Norton & Co, London 1990.

Index